# Doomsday: Dark Sage

## Stuart France & Sue Vincent

..."Ah, but Little Grub, the lost stone of Chat may well still be found."
"O Something Feral, not within the pages of 'The Ætheling Thing' it won't."
"Well, there's always the next book."

Wen smiles, takes another copious bite out of her Bake-Well Tart and starts munching on it.

Break-Fast she calls it!

Like normal people ever have Bakewell Tart for Breakfast....

*Book Two of the Doomsday Triad*

# Doomsday:
## Dark Sage

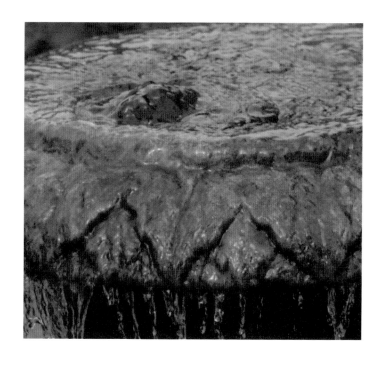

Stuart France & Sue Vincent

For Ned and Vee and the Folk of Faerie

# Contents

...Until the time of the number of Melchizedek,
the great Receiver of light came to purify those powers...

.

# Introduction:

'Joseph of Arimathea a wealthy Metal Merchant first traded here for lead and copper from Priddy and Green Ore in the Mendips, and for tin from Cornwall.

The two former would ship from Pilton's Harbour which was situated just below where the present Manor House stands and on the way out to sea, he would pass Glastonbury, then an island south-west of Pylle Bay.

After our Lord's ascension and Pentecost, Joseph would naturally return to preach the Gospel to his old friends here and at Glastonbury and to build a wattle church at each place.

Here, he built a chapel on the side of the hill above the harbour, where probably he baptised his first converts.'

- *Traditional History of Pilton Church.*

"Does the Pope know about this," says Wen, her eyes alight, "I can't believe it's so brazenly presented and on an information board as well."
"We may be able to do even better than that," say I contemplating the church banner with some interest.
"How so?" says Wen.
"Well if the line of the Tor depicted here is correct, it shouldn't be too difficult to locate the precise spot where they first touched down."
"No," says Wen suddenly collapsing into fits of laughter. "No it can't be that accurate can it? It is probably done by the local kids. And how would they know anyway?"
"It wasn't done by the local kids."
"How do you know?"
"I know because the colour symbolism is too precise."
"You may have to qualify that last statement Mr Sams," says Wen with something of a crooked grin.
"Not hard," say I. "The figure in the prow of the vessel adorned by a golden halo, which for arguments sake we will call 'Jesus,' is wearing a purple robe."

"He is," says Wen.

"The older child who is steering the boat is wearing a purple tunic."

"He is too. Do we have a name for him?" says Wen.

"I could quite easily give him a name if you would like me to?"

"I am sure you could but that is not quite the same thing. What does the tradition call him?"

"The tradition doesn't call him anything but if I had to have a wild stab in the dark at what it would call him if asked, I'd say it would call him 'John'."

"Oh you would, would you? Isn't he a bit too old for John?"

"We've already established that John was at least two years older than Jesus."

"Okay... and the older figure of course we know only too well from the tradition?"

"And Our Joseph just happens to be wearing a purple head-dress?"

Wen looks from figure to figure and back to me and then moves up close to scrutinise the line and angle of the Tor depicted in the background.

"It's worth a go," she says and raises her camera.

***

'The concept of 'darkness' was revealing.
It is where light ends. But I also realised that darkness is not the absence of light but the antithesis of light. In other words, they are aspects of each other. Light and dark are not only metaphors but the means by which we perceive and understand.'

-   *Vittorio Storaro*

# Chapter One:
## *Devil's-Drop*

"...Mum! Dad! Don't touch it! It's EVIL!" – *Kevin from 'Time Bandits'.*

Figure 1 – *'Death on a Bi-Cycle...'*

"He says he wants to investigate my vision."

"Who does?"

"You haven't been listening to a word I've been saying."

"Oh Ned, you mean...well, what you have to ask yourself is, do you really want your vision investigating?"

"I'm not sure."

"Or even, does your vision want your vision investigating?"

"I'm not sure I even know what he means by my vision."

"Presumably he's referring to all those stories you make up."

"But he hasn't read any of those stories and I don't make them up," says Wen, reaching for her Gazetteer of Mysterious Britain and brandishing it.

"I know you don't, dear, I'm just teasing. Vee has read them though and she's probably told him all about it, or at least enough to get him interested and you *were* dancing with him in Oxford last May Day."

"Yeah, that's true I was dancing with him, him and about thirty other people also. I think *he* thinks I'm still working in Buckinghamshire."

"He's in for a nasty surprise then..."

"If he does agree to come up here do we take him to Devil's Drop?"

"We could, it would certainly make for an interesting experiment but we would have to give him some sort of warning if we did."

Devil's Drop is our new name for Gib-Rock.

Wen has been doing some more research on the story and I have to say, our theories on legend notwithstanding, the bare facts of this one alone are rapidly approaching mythological proportions.

Get this...

On the way to the gibbet the cart carrying the body got lost and had to pass over the territory now known to us fondly as Chat. Now, at that time there was not actually a thoroughfare over the land, but passage to the dead has to be given when requested.

"Why does passage to the dead have to be given when requested?"

"It's an Old English Custom."

"It becomes a law simply because people are accustomed to doing it?"

"Don't you just love it?"

"It's utterly bonkers but beautiful!"

"It's nothing less than a road of the dead."

"The road that passes through Chat is a Corpse Road."

"I mean this is quite recent, yeah, within living memory?"

"It was in the Eighteenth century, so *almost* within living memory."

"I think that's part of an older tale that has got mixed up with an actual occurrence. It could only happen in Derbyshire."

"Is that also why huge standing stones as big as any you've ever seen also go missing there?"

I have to say that the last remark was a little below the belt...

***

"If you sit with your back to the Telling Stone of Bar-Brook One, just as your Feathered Seer, or whatever it is you're now calling her was wont to do..."

"She's called Bratha!"

"Bratha, yes, that's right."

"It means Knowledge."

"Is that knowledge with a capital 'K' or with a small 'k'?"

Wen smiles...

"Anyway if you sit with your back to the Telling Stone of Bar-Brook One looking out over the Moor to the horizon at midwinter sunset... the sun sets into Arbor Low and Arbor Low, as we now know, is a Serpent Temple which at its inception would have housed at least seventy-two recumbent stones."

"At least seventy-two?" smiles Wen.

"I'm counting some of the gaps there now obviously."

"That's Egyptian."

"You'd have thought so wouldn't you?"

"It's the underworld conceived as the snake Apep."

"And it could be argued that it is also the seventy-two names of God which are the nine personality types on the ring of shadow finally self-assessed."

"So did the Egyptians come here?"

"Or did whoever was here go to Egypt?"

"Strange how the self-same questions keep popping up..."

"...In totally different contexts."

"Moses came out of Egypt. Jesus fled there. Even Pythagoras was reputed to have studied in the Egyptian Mystery Schools."

"And as a Social Python, 'he' is another snake."

"Whenever you make mention of recumbent stones I can't help thinking of the stars."

"Oh, it was a Star-Temple too, I just haven't got around to mapping the stones onto the stars that would have been overhead at the time yet that's all."

"Poor Ned," smiles Wen, "I wonder what he'll make of it all?"

*\*\*\**

Figure 2 – '*Cloak of Rocks...*'

...“Why would a Saint want to wear a Cloak of Rocks?”
Ned and I are contemplating the stained glass depiction of St. Andrew at the
St Nicholas Church of High Bradfield.
“That's no cloak,” says Ned. “That's a fish net.”
“Whoa,” say I.
“Whoa?” says Ned.
“That may just mean that the Saint Andrew of Scotland and Andrew, the
disciple of Christ are in actual fact one and the same personage!”
“Whoa,” says Ned.
“I know,” say I. “St Andrew, the fisher of men.”
“Or boys,” says Ned with a crooked smile and indicates the foreground
figure, “Is that an allusion to the miracle of the loaves and the fishes, there are
five loaves and two fishes.”
“Oh Lord,” say I. “Don't get me started on geometry.”

*** 

Ben takes a long draw on his cigar, leans back somewhat unsteadily in his
metallic garden chair and blows the smoke high into the night air.

“You look like Puff the Magic Dragon,” smiles Wen.
 Ben starts to giggle immoderately, “Yes, oh yes, I remember him...”

Ben launches into an impromptu rendition of the song gets halfway through
the chorus forgets the words and then starts to giggle immoderately again...
As may have been already surmised, the second of our Glastonbury talks
went a lot better than the first.

Now, there may have been a number of reasons for this and not all of them
may be reasons which we would have guessed at the time or indeed really
wanted but for the moment at least we are happy in the afterglow of a job
well done and it means we can look forward with a certain amount of gusto
to our next workshop in Derbyshire which is only a week away.

Wen gives me one of her ‘hit him with the diagram’ looks and I duly oblige.

“What's this,” says Ben rocking back to the table on his metallic garden chair,

"The... Doy...Da's... Cauldron... foaming, ah, yes I remember this too," he says, squinting at the pair of us through a grey plume of cigar smoke. "Thought you could catch me out did you, you naughty people."

"So what's it about then?" laughs Wen.

Ben pauses, looks at me and then looks at Wen, looks back to the diagram shakes his head and says, "I have absolutely no idea whatsoever, please proceed with your doubtlessly fascinating account of the third of our Four Talismans."

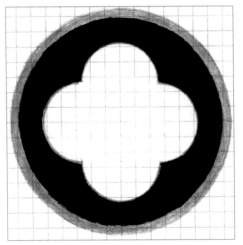

Figure 3 – *'Dagda's Cauldron – Foaming...'*

"At least he's accepted them as ours now," says Wen.

"The Dagda's cauldron is infinite Being," say I.

"No eye that spies it remains unsatisfied," says Wen.

"But of course it is," says Ben. "And of course it doesn't. I knew that. Why, why...it's just what I've been trying to teach all along."

\*\*\*

...Maybe it is because it is our third visit or maybe it is because there are three of us, or maybe we had to work out the St Andrew thing before we were allowed to ascend, who knows? Whatever the reasons, we re-convene on top of the man-made-conical-mound which hides behind the Church of St Nicholas, High Bradfield and Wen has an interesting take on proceedings.

"If St Andrew of Scotland is Andrew the Disciple of Christ then he may have come over here with Joseph of Arimathea."

"And remember at that time there was no Scotland. Scotland was North Albion!"

"North Albion," smiles Wen. "I like that."

"Why *did* they come here?" says Ned.

"If we knew that..." say I.

"If we knew that, then what?" says Wen.

"If we knew that for sure, we'd probably all be millionaires," say I somewhat wishfully.

"Not necessarily," says Ned, who may already be a millionaire for all I know. "After all this time, nobody is really all that interested."

"That's true enough."

"It would still be nice to know though."

"Why does anyone go anywhere?" say I. "Why do people go to Glastonbury? Why do people come here now? They're still doing it. Why?"

"They come because they're called," says Ned simply.

The Call of Albion:

And then a still silence descends
Upon our three-fold gathering
And we look out to the far horizon
Each of us from a slightly different angle
To where the mists are gathering form
And preparing to roll in to greet us one and all...

\*\*\*

As a special treat for Ned we agree to take him to see the Venerable Mr Fox who, we have been reliably informed, will be dancing, along with his enigmatic troop of vermin in Holmfirth this evening. But before we set out Ned wants to change out of his sodden clothes and brush himself up a little so we retire, each to our separate domiciles and Wen and I get down to a little research...

"There's no mention of Andrew in the Arimathean entourage. In fact there's no mention of any of the disciples. It *is* the five loaves and two fishes in the foreground of the window though, apparently, Andrew found the lad and presented him to the Lord before the miracle was performed."

Figure 4 – '*Over-Kill-Hill...*'

"I didn't realise that," say I pensively. "It seems a little odd if he did indeed come here... What?"

"I can see you thinking it but don't say it!"

"Okay, I won't but there's more to this fish story than meets the eye, what with the inclusion of the Saltire and all."

"St Andrew's relics are in Scotland, I mean North Albion, but his ministry was in central Europe; Poland, that sort of area."

"So how did his relics end up here?"

"A shipwreck washed them ashore."

"You know the more I hear from the Roman perspective, the less I believe but at least it gives us an excuse to go to Scotland."

"Woo Hoo..." says Wen and punches the air "finally!"

She seems quite pleased.

The weather though is rather less pleasing. It has been raining on and off since we first entered the Circle on Hordron's Edge and as we set out for Holmfirth the rain sets in good and proper.

"Any chance the Foxes won't dance tonight?" asks Ned.
"There is absolutely no chance whatsoever of the Foxes not dancing tonight."

*\*\*\**

Where do they come from?
They come out of the night.

Where do they go to?
Back to the night they return.

They dance in the dark
To pipe and drum and fiddle.

They dance in the dark,
With fire and brandished flame.

Nobody knows who they are...

- *The Langsett Foxes*

*\*\*\**

Ned seems to be enjoying himself which is something of a relief. It is hard to know what people expect and Ned has passed up an opportunity to be taking part in a whole weekend of temple rituals... to be outside with us!

"To be outside with us in the rain," adds Wen.

Thankfully, one does not notice the rain when the Langsett Foxes dance which is just as well because it well and truly pours down when they are on. Ned is so impressed he is all for shipping an entourage of them out to the U.S. for a stint so they can pass on their skills if he could have found any of them to ask after the dance.

He is big on not letting crafts and traditions die out and he is right to be so concerned. It is one of the things that can happen when one moves away from traditionally oriented life styles and ultimately it is dangerous.

We call in at a pub for a final 'salvo' before retiring and have to hole up in the back room to avoid the noise from the fifties music. The people twisting and turning and jiving and rocking around the clock in the front room of the pub probably range from between fifteen to twenty-five years older than me. It seems strange that these things come in waves or pulses which are translated into phases by people and which those people can then never really forget.

Music it has been claimed is our most reliable way of predicting the future.

"Will it still be raining tomorrow?"

I sincerely hope not.

***

Thankfully the day starts bright and sunny and we get to spend a pleasant hour or so after picking Ned up from The Psalter, in Eccles-Hall Woods alongside the Wood Stone.

Ned endears himself to us still further by not dismissing our somewhat controversial theories with regard to the stone but in some ways that proves even more frustrating because if it is a 3D model of a nearby landscape, which Wen and I firmly believe it is, then we have still not really got anywhere near finding it.

"Wen does have and always has had a pet theory on that score, but let's not go there, just yet."
"Where to next then?" says Wen giving me a look.
"Oh I don't know, how about...Arbor Low?"
"Arbor Low it is then!"

***

As we commence the now familiar walk up to the farm and the donation tin by the gate, the clouds again start to gather. It is always windy up here but couple that wind with rain and you have probably got a recipe for a fairly uncomfortable sojourn in the Stone Henge of the North.

And that is precisely what we get except if anything the rain falls hard enough to be regarded as personal.

"Maybe we should be asking permission before we enter?" says Ned.

I shake my head and smile but it is hard to know why we do not have to do that. This can happen in the circles partly because, according to some sources, one of their functions was weather control but it has to be owned that the downpours have been particularly virulent and do seem to have been timed to perfection for our entry and exit from the stones.

Wen has started calling Ned, 'The Rain Man'.

Ned just wants to take some of it home to America where they are having something of a drought. It is a tad annoying though, not least because we are not able to spend as long as we would have liked at the sites and Ned is not really getting to see them in their best light. Not that he seems to mind. He has already told us that he got more than he could have expected up on Hordron's Edge and that was even before we had got him into one of the circles proper. The other annoying thing is that when it does then stop raining the sun comes out and absolutely blazes. Presumably you have heard of April showers, well these are May cloud-bursts. Again, Ned seems unfazed. He pronounces himself well pleased with the Stone Henge of the North and the way Wen is able to skip from site to site so nonchalantly without so much as a glance at a map and that is what finally decides us.

"We've just been toying with you so far," says Wen, "with all this weather and all."
Which of course is not strictly true, "Yeah, we've been seeing if you're ready for the ultimate test."
"The ultimate test?" says Ned.
"Devil's Drop," say I, "It's EVIL!"

"Lead on," says Ned after a suitably dramatic pause for reflection.

\*\*\*

"It doesn't look much from a distance," say I.

"Oh I don't know," says Ned, "But why the Devil's Drop?"

"Well, it started out as Devil's Rock because of a perceived likeness, in our minds at least, to Devil's Tower, Wyoming," says Wen.

"But of course it's nowhere near as big as the Devil's Tower," say I.

"And the evil bit?"

"Well, we had a bit of a... what shall we say, we had a bit of a strange experience up there when we tried to climb it, didn't we Wen?"

This is an awful cop out I know but if the truth be told there are two emotions at play here vying for precedence. The first is a feeling of foolishness because from this distance at the side of the road the 'Drop' looks like nothing more than a rather impressive and undoubtedly fascinating natural rock formation, whilst the second is the memory of the experience I had when climbing it which latter has been impinging itself ever since we turned the Silver Bullet in its general direction and it has become abundantly clear that we are indeed seriously considering the utter madness of taking Ned 'up the Drop'.

"That's right," says Wen gamely, "We think there's a warding up there, but we'd like a second opinion."

"You've both been up, right?" says Ned.

"I've been up there," I say quietly. "Wen ran away."

"I did not run away, Donald Sams..." says Wen. "I merely moved away rapidly in the opposite direction... and anyway... you never got to the top."

"I did *so* get to the top I just never stood up on the top that's all."

"Never stood up?" says Ned.

"For fear of being blown off."

"Was it windy?"

"Not particularly."

"I see," smiles Ned.

"I'm not sure you do. It's the Devil's Drop: it's EVIL!"

\*\*\*

The thing is, there is so much more we could have told Ned and perhaps should have told him. The latest batch of research has thrown up image after image of doom in the form of stretchers and ambulances at the site. At least three climbers have fallen from the top in recent memory. How many more previously it would be difficult to say. Still, he has been warned and he does not have to go up. We prepare for our ascent, in silence, by donning waterproofs and just to emphasise the ridiculous nature of our climate in 'good old Albion' when we are done a couple a joggers strut past in t-shirt and shorts.

Of course if the 'Rain Man' runs true to form we will be approaching the drop in a torrential downpour.

We have to descend into the valley before we can get onto the right track and fortunately Wen takes over and fills the silence, by explaining the links between the college site of Arbor Low and this place. We rest up at the bottom of the valley and Wen points out the caves which she believes were an integral part of the inevitable initiations which took place at the site.

Even from this distance, and we are now quite close, the rock appears to all intents and purposes benign, but when we hit the track there comes a point, and Wen and I both feel it, when you just *know*. We rest up for Wen to take some shots and if Ned is having second thoughts about getting up there now would be the time to confess them.

I look at Ned intending to put the question but Ned has gone grey.

"The Devil's Drop: it's EVIL!" I say.

If Ned *is* having second thoughts Wen is having none of it and she finishes up snapping and immediately charges off left of the track up the steepest part of the Mother Rock that spawned the Drop.

This, I was not expecting... she is moving at pace and if she attempts the climb in that frame of mind she may well become another casualty so I charge after her, leaving Ned to his own devices. As I slip by the edge of the rock a cast back reveals Ned angling towards the other side of the Drop but Wen is already approaching the channel I used to get up last time so I redouble my efforts to catch her.

'First she runs away then she charges', I keep thinking as I reach the bottom of the channel. I know now for sure that there is absolutely no danger in the climb up the channel and this allows me to be somewhat unconcerned as I look up and see Wen grappling with the peak of the ascent.

Figure 5 – *'Devil's Spawn.'*

She is furiously intent on the climb and the intensity of her features brings back memories of my first ascent. I eventually draw level with her position and have to admit that although the channel has this time held few if any terrors for me I still have little desire to climb up onto the top.

"Can you see Ned?"
"Didn't he follow you?"
"No, he went off up the other side, I think."

Wen manoeuvres herself carefully into a position that allows her to peer cautiously over the edge of the 'Drop'.

"Can't see him," she yells even though I am only inches from her face, and then shudders.
"Come on," say I, "there's no reason to stay up here any longer than we have to."

We meet up with Ned at about the point on our descent that we all split up.

He claims to have got up the other side but without examining the rock it would be impossible to say whether he has or not.

Wen keeps casting vicious looks back up at the rock which I explain is *not* the best way to go.

"It's Devil's Drop," says Ned. "It's EVIL, but we overcame it!"

High Fives all around and Big Hugs...one to each... and each to the other.

\*\*\*

**Chapter Two:**

# *Soul Dreaming*

'You are Horus, son of Hathor, to whom was shown a decapitated body. Your head will not be taken from you.'– *Land of the Exiles.*

Figure 6 - 'Field of Dreams...'

We had stared for a while beforehand, for hours, perhaps?

We had talked about how good it would be, if only we could have found the way.

The outhouses had been good initially, but they were only small and smelled a lot and it was too dark to see anything when once you were inside; but getting in, actually breaking in had been fun and that was all that really mattered...

...And now this.

It really would be something if we could get inside here!
This place would be different.
This place would be better.
We would be able to see inside here because it was so huge, this place was enormous!
We had searched for the way, an entrance overlooked, forgotten, but there was nothing like that... No loosely boarded windows or half bolted doors that could more easily have been forced, no rusting padlock hanging loose... there was nothing!
Maybe... we were not supposed to get into this place.
None of us believed that.
We considered the drains and sewers, looked up to the roof and then resumed our search until eventually we came to stare, unspeaking, at a loose brick which the smallest of us had kicked in desperation.
We all knew then that we had found the way.
We knew but still we stared, hardly daring to believe what had been asked of us.
We could not demolish a building brick by brick when we were so small and the building was so huge, the builders even huger.
How could we do that?
How could we even contemplate setting about such a task?
Somebody kicked the brick again and a puff of cement billowed airily in the breeze...
Undoubtedly we would still have been discussing matters now had I not fetched my mallet and my chisel.
A heavy, rusty iron mallet and a thick, heavy, rusty iron chisel.

Both implements were draped with dust laden spider-webs... both were lying at the bottom of a warped, rusty metal bucket, the bent handle of which groaned agonisingly when moved.

I had taken them surreptitiously when I had not really needed stealth... and then I had run, with the mallet a heavy lump of eagerness and the chisel, hard, enthusiasm; both implements protruded out of the top of my trousers and jabbed the pit of my stomach, hurting me I was so excited... and all the time thinking, thinking... had I not done that then they would still have been staring, just as they stared anyway; watching me, dumbfounded and scared, spellbound by the clang of metal on stone which bounced off all the walls, creating a sound which became the ringing in my mind, a sound to which only I was accustomed...

*** 

The seeing stone is chill against my spine as I wait for the dawn.
Their shades are close this night.
They are Wakeful.
I hear their whispers on the wind as the shift comes and I find them across the ages.

...She paints his eyes, smearing shimmering colour across the lids with gilded fingers. They work in silence in the yellow false-light. Garbed in black, they are not themselves. I feel them, yet something else overlays them, shadowing forth into the world; latent, coming, but not yet...not yet.

He leaves the place where she did not sleep; she looks into the cold surface that hangs like ice upon the wall, seeing other souls not her own. She is many, she is Three. I look through her eyes, as she looks through mine... seer and priestess... and the 'Other'.

We are the Three that are 'One'.

Painted eyes stare back, black rimmed. About her neck a heavy collar, she is crowned and winged with gold and power, girdled with stars. She steps back into the shadow of herself, opens her heart and I feel the shift once more, this time through her. It is time.

\*\*\*

...But of course there was no one to hear the sound of demolition on a demolition site and when nobody came they all joined in. They were safe after all and they grabbed pieces of metal and long sticks and large stones, jemmied, struck, forced and kicked, tugged and waggled until the brick came away and I fell back onto the concrete, my face, white and gritty, and trickling dirt, the brick still clasped in my hand, grasped tight for I would never let go of that first brick. I cast it away; watched it break in two upon impact with the ground and then laughed at the small square space which had been created in the corner of the building.

The brick had been extracted as if it were a tooth and a stream of cold air flowed out from within, flowed out as a warning but it was too late, they were attacking the rest of the corner. I need do no more for a little while so I lay back and looked at the sun, listened to the grunts and gasps, the squabbles and yelps and the dull thud of their blows as they worked; those sounds made pleasant by my contemplative mood. Eventually there was silence and I looked up to find them staring mute questions at my prostrate form.

The job was complete. They were scared again. They had realised the outcome of their labour and they did not like it. It was not fun anymore. They were after all, only children. They looked shamefacedly at the remains of their ferocity, their madness, their desire... The bricks were strewn in a wide radius about them, some broken in half, nearly all of them chipped and battered, others completely smashed.

Their faces wore expressions of utter incomprehension and from there they turned to the smallish gap destroyed in the wall. It was a gap just big enough for a small man to crawl through. The dust of their endeavour had not yet settled and they stood looking dishevelled and forlorn amid its disseminating form.

They had, of course, only been acting upon orders but I had given none and this they understood as they gaped, alone and frightened.

The silence of their words drifted, for they spoke in minutes now and each of them in turn dropped their makeshift tools, the metal bar clanking, sadly and emptily, on the concrete, a lifeless rattle now that a crime had been uncovered.

I stood, and smiling, slowly walked across to them.

They were eagerness itself now and clamoured around me, babbling and laughing in nervous relief.

"That was great fun Sam, it really was... but... "

"It's very dark inside... "

"And cold... "

"It's impossible to make anything out... "

"There could be something in there... "

"There could be anything in there... Anything... at all... "

"And it's a very small hole... a very tight fit."

"Very tight... what if we get stuck?"

"What if we get in but we can't get out?" ...

***

Figure 7 – 'The Crown...'

...Their world seems strange to me... all sharp angles and smooth walls reflecting light, yet I read it through her, know its ways somehow. It is stranger still on *this* dawning when they have brought the ancient into the new...

...She knocks on the wood that hangs in a portal, three times. It is opened by the Green Man, robed in white and veiled, hooded perhaps, I do not know. His eyes show fear and his breath is sharp, ragged as she summons him to his death.

Down they walk, he behind she. He is strange to me, this other one. Yet I know him, he too is of the three and power flows between.

They enter a closed space, dimly lit with flames in the circle. The other one is there, yet he too is 'Other', robed in midnight, tall as the trees and masked... a black beast with golden eyes. They stand silent in the circle... three, six and nine I see, all the levels of their being that wait in abeyance while others come in.

Black remains to call them to the rite, one by one. Gold and Green face the morning, walking silent through stone to the hillside starred with swallow-flowers and wet with dew. Higher they climb to the mound that looks out across the valley. Shaped like a tomb, a place of death in life and life in death. Beside them is a tree... and on it a crown of thorns.

She binds him; the black cords of death that tie him to life, the cords of life that tie him to the Mother. In his hands a crystal like the moon and at his feet the crown and the waiting earth. Power flows, around and between, cloaking them in its mists from the eyes of the profane. Eyes lock and she raises her wings, golden in the morning, taking him into her silence.

The Black Jackal, cloaked in night leads them to the rite, a dark snake of figures huddled against the chill of a spring dawn. Their garb is strange, the colours of summer flowers, stark against the green. They walk in silence as the Black One opens the way for them to pass. Higher still until they reach the mound and there they wait, looking up.

Figure 8 – *'The Mound of Becoming...'*

He circles, prowling the bounds of the sacred space, marking the circle with his footsteps in the dew, once around, bowing as she turns, revealing the Green Man to the Companions.

The Jackal climbs the mound and Black and Gold salute each other, sparking lines of power crackle silently between them, bright white and gold, seen only through a seer's eyes. They bow to the immobile, verdant form, locked in the lightless stasis of death until his heart is opened.

The Black one speaks out "Let the star rise, let the flame leap!"

His voice shatters the silence, opening the way on yet another level. The Golden One takes the crystal from the heart of the Green Man, raising it to the Sun, "Ours if the heart is wise, to take… and to keep!"

As she speaks the sphere is returned, earth to earth accepted, while the Green Man stands empty.

On each side of him they stand as pillars of light and darkness. Deeper I look and see them night and day, the birthing of the golden sun held in the heart of darkness, the shadow of its death cased in gold. Three that are 'One', inextricable, interdependent for their being, and purpose, while overhead the Hawk flies free.

One by one they come, called by the staff of the Jackal, close in his shadowed Light, held in his cloak. Softly he whispers to each of their destiny, of the Hawk that waits in their hearts, anointing them with fragrant oil that fills the morning with perfume. The Golden One takes them into her wings and as they pass before the Green Man they are held, poised between Light and Dark as they bow and gaze at the earth-held crystal, into the Heart of the Rose.

The Golden Mother blesses them with the warmth of touch on each heart and the promise of life on her lips. From the heart of the Green One she takes a heart, entrusting it to their keeping, a symbol of awakening to Light and Life. Eyes meet eyes, heart meets heart, and life touches Life. Clasping the symbol they move beyond, standing on the other side of death… a true initiation for those who can encompass it.

But one remains; the silent sacrifice, bound and immobile in the frozen morning. Black and Gold they turn to him. The Walker between the Worlds anoints his brow and, holding his eyes whispers his journey to the stars, the Mother warms his heart and with her touch come the words of life. He cries out, the Father who is the Son, like a babe's first breath, wakened from death to the life of the heart.

It is done. Golden wings enfold him, shrouding him in Light and one by one they leave the hillside silent, the rite accomplished.

Three remain, silent still, feet wet with dew. Three are quiescent, watching their Selves. The Three remain Other and holding the power for what is to come. Nine that are Three that are One.

… And I, shivering in the rain-damp morning against the Telling Stone, miles and ages apart, I am their witness.

\*\*\*

"It *is* magic," says Wen.

"What is?" say I.

"Your Man thing," says Wen.

"I beg your pardon?"

"The incredible appearing and disappearing island," says Wen.

"Oh *that*. What do you mean?"

"It's an optical illusion."

"I thought you said it was magic," say I.

"That's science's term for magic," says Wen.

"Can we start again please, I'm confused," say I.

"It is one of the following; a Superior Mirage, a Refractive Looming, a Refractive Towering or a Fata Morgana."

"Is this supposed to be making things clearer?"

"And you were right it does have to do with the weather conditions."

"I wish I was reassured. I am usually only too happy to be right."

"Pick one!" says Wen.

"Pick one what?" say I.

"One of the following: a Superior Mirage, a Refractive Looming, a Refractive Towering or a Fata Morgana."

"Okay," say I, "I'll have a Superior Mirage."

"I knew you would but you're wrong!"

"How do you know I'm wrong?"

"Because your Isle wasn't upside down was it?"

"No, my isle wasn't upside down."

"And it would have been if it had been a Superior Mirage. It would also have been in the sky, and not in the sea, that's the superior bit."

"It was definitely in the sea and not in the sky."

"Pick another," says Wen who is clearly enjoying herself.

"Okay," say I, "I'll have a Fata Morgana."

"I just knew you'd go for that second but you're wrong again."

Wen can be incredibly infuriating at times.

"How do you know I'm wrong?" I say with some exasperation.

"Because your isle didn't have towers and colonnades did it?"

"No, my isle didn't have towers and colonnades," say I resignedly.

"So it wasn't a Fata Morgana," says Wen.

"Is all this for real?" say I. "Science has actually catalogued all this."

"Oh yes," says Wen happily. "It's for real alright."

"Does Morgy know she's named after an illusion?"

"Probably, but not quite in that sense. Pick another."

"Seeing as you, 'just know' what I'm going to pick next anyway, why don't you pick one for me?"

"Okay," says Wen, "you'll have a Refractive Looming and you're wrong again!"

"Unbelievable," say I. "Why am I wrong this time?"

"Because you'd have to be out at sea and looking out over the horizon for it to have been a Refractive Looming."

"Which leaves?"

"Which leaves a Refractive Towering," says Wen.

"Which is?" say I.

"Which is an elongation of the perceived object caused by the refraction of light when a layer of warm air settles on a layer of cold air at sunset."

"There was a storm later that night," say I.

"There you go then, that's your Refractive Towering alright."

"You can just imagine what the ancients would have made of it."

"We don't need to imagine," says Wen. "We know what they made of it."

"Yes," say I somewhat wistfully, "I suppose we do."

"Hy Brasil," says Wen.

"Ultima Thule," say I.

"Abellach," says Wen.

"Hyper Boreas," say I.

They made of it a life at rainbow's end!

\*\*\*

# Chapter Three:
## *The Hooded Stone*

'But if our gospel is hid it is hid to those who are lost...' – *2 Cor. 4:3*

Figure 9 – *'Verdant Green.'*

...My friends melted away beside me and my eyes widened and grew accustomed to the darkness beyond as it brightened into a grey, sandy crevice threatening to split in two one of the sun-cracked slats forming the wooden steps which led to and from the beach and the lower promenade of White-Lake sea front...

Thirty minutes earlier the retreating fizz of mucky foam had deposited a star fish, translucent and fleshy, pink and squelchy, onto the greasy surface of the wet wood but now the blub of dead sea-life has shrunk and curled into the brittle, five-fold splash of tiny orange peel craters which were once so familiar to anyone walking the shoreline. I am five years old and after two tentative, unyielding finger pokes to banish the lingering fear of a sting I pick up the fish and hurtle prom-wards to exhibit my find.

As I get there, but before my father tells me to throw the fish over the prom-rails and back onto the beach below because it is dead and dirty I hear the clearing of phlegm from a throat and I turn to find Bill Bell-shank gobbing out a comet tailed globule of chocolate streaked spittle. As the projectile lurches out over the prom rail a gust of wind blows it back shore-wards, eliciting a yell of laughter as Bill dodges its wayward course onto the wet tarmac which covers the swell of the cliff-top widening to embrace the colonnades and arches of the Metro-Pole car-park beyond. Bill's face is red from the exhilaration of riding against the wind, and of the last steep climb to the Pier front. Bill is seventeen years old and it is just weeks before his nose is transformed into a crimson limbed Octopus in a fight with one of the Robinson twins. He is months away from the car crash which will draw a dull veil of incomprehension across his eyes when we meet, and we are still a couple of years away from Bill's detention for persistently following Madeline on her way to and from her place of work. As he clamps his bike lock around the promenade rail and through the spokes of his back wheel and turns to head for the amusement arcade where we enjoy a successful night, I fail to follow, for the panting breath I can hear, louder than the wind comes from over my shoulder and there it echoes about the vaults of the alcoves above the paint-peeled arches of the colonnades.

Madeline lies beneath me and the night air is cold on the small of my exposed back as we rock and rock together and then I collapse as we burst simultaneously into fits of laughter. As she moves off along the promenade on a walk home during which we are destined to argue for no other reason than that we are both drunk, I turn and walk towards the Cenotaph leaving Madeline to a future in which at least one of her children is not mine. I am twenty-five years old and for the first time in my life I have pondered the nature and effects of a structural edifice which should be as familiar to me as my own name.

The drooping chains of black iron which surround the depression of bedded banks and which circle the stone obelisk, part in an entrance slope which allows my passage to its three-tiered base. The bronze relief of uniformed figures at war leads my gaze upwards onto block after block of huge yellow stone which pivot away into swirling black and form a jaundiced, geometrical finger, pointing out the stars.

The names of the dead we are not supposed to forget have been engraved on a plaque too high to be read from the ground...

\*\*\*

..."Okay," says Wen, "that sounds infinitely do-able."

It may be my imagination but her tone has something steely and determined about it. Maybe it is the thought of our escapade the last time we went in search of the stone? No one really enjoys mud sliding fully clothed however much they may protest otherwise at the time. Still, it will be good to re-visit some old haunts, the plan is a sound one and the disappearance of the stone in such spectacular circumstances has been bugging me for some time. I like to pride myself on my memory and for it to be so woefully found wanting is disconcerting to say the least.

It will though be strange leaving the Silver Bullet. But leaving the facilitator of our adventures will be something of an adventure in itself and also something of a throw-back to former times when this was the only way I could get into the landscape. Besides, we are supposed to be re-tracing the steps of that day so many years ago when quite by chance Ali and Sal and I stumbled upon the dark stone looming black and magnificent in the corner of a field. We had travelled by bus from the Field of Sheaves then but at least today we would not be boarding the bus until halfway through our journey, at Baslow.

Wen parks up the Silver Bullet and we sit, musing upon Ben's latest blog-post whilst we wait for the bus. His versions of the events that we have shared together are always interesting and today's description of our visit to Devil's Drop makes fascinating reading.

The bus arrives pretty much on time but then immediately starts to lose time through a combination of cyclists on the road and the inevitable weekend traffic trying to get to and through Bakewell.

It is so long ago since I was last at Beeley that we almost miss the stop and as we run back into the village square we are met with the first disappointment.

"They've done up the pub!"

The Devonshire Arms, Beeley is no longer a warm and friendly village pub but has instead become an à la carte bar–cum–restaurant, replete with a line of four by four vehicles blocking its still quaintly picturesque exterior. I cast a forlorn look into my old corner by the fire which now has a long table crammed into it and sidle over to the bar in some trepidation.

"They don't even serve stout!"

So we sit outside for a spell mulling over our drinks, bemoaning the loss of culture and the inevitable but soon to be negotiated climb up through the wood and out onto the High Moor.

Our second disappointment proves to be the current incumbent of the bench surrounding the Old Yew outside the parish church which means that we cannot spend any time there and have to settle instead for a hastily framed shot of the tree from one angle only.

These old, old trees are without question an important and wholly integral part of the sacredness of our churchyards and time spent in their company is never time wasted. Still, time is moving on as it always does and we have a steep climb and a long walk ahead of us...

*\*\**

...Ned is taking the triumph of Devil's Drop rather well and insists that we visit one of *his* old haunts from when he was last over in Derbyshire for the 'Alchemy One' Workshop.

The Public House that he takes us to turns out to be more House than Public and is also worryingly close to the road that runs past the, '...Drop'. Still, I force such minor details to the back of my mind along with the Public House sign which consists of three skeletal stag heads mounted on the white-washed outside wall and boldly enter the fray in Ned's wake.

"It is a pub for those who work the land not those who own the land," Vee would say much later and this description would have been reassuring at this point in the proceedings had I been aware of it at the time.

Wen and I manage to find a corner table which does not have a greyhound standing on it and before we have time to fully digest the stuffed and standing rabbit in the window which appears to be carrying a rifle, an over-large pint jug of Black Lurcher and a bottle of alcoholic Dandelion and Burdock materialise on the table in front of us. Ned disappears into the back room moments before the folk band strike up and my mind returns again to our proximity to the '...Drop'. I can't help thinking about a series of folk stories known as 'The Grateful Dead.'

The locals though prove friendly enough and before long we are chatting to Andrew the landlord as he takes us through the intricacies and peculiarities of his collection of animal skulls and fossil stones which he keeps on show at the back of the bar.

Ned returns from the back room all too soon and as we regain our place in the corner to finish our drinks he solemnly and somewhat forcibly announces that he is ready for one more.

He is referring to Stone Circles and that can only mean one thing.

I look at Wen and Wen looks at me and we both know what the other is thinking.

'Barbrook One!'

\*\*\*

...Clouds hang heavy over the moor, it has rained, heavily, and the ground is soaked. Bracken and heather-fall carpets the paths, drinking the water like a sponge until saturation. Brackish puddles mirror an ominous sky as we guide our visitor to the Telling Stone.

I point out the plateau where the old ones had lived.

"That's where the goats were kept."

There is no smoke in my vision today, no fire…

As always the stone looks bigger as we approach; as if the distance allows us to see what *is,* and proximity only that small part of what it is that we perceive.

It feels like coming home to an empty house.

We climb the short rise to the circle. I lay my hand on the stone and feel grief well up inside me. It is like touching a tombstone, though she does not lie here. Not far though…I squat against the stone. *Her* place… in the silence of bereavement…

\*\*\*

...As we start to climb a few specks of rain begin to fall from the leaden sky and I feel justified in my choice of apparel. It is only later that I begin to regret the Wellington boots.

A third disappointment looms at the farmyard at the foot of the wood. Where once there were turkeys and peacocks and cockatoos there is… nothing… the yard is empty, bereft of all life. It is a further insult to my memory, somehow. I suppose I am still thinking of this when I take a wrong turn into the wood and that particular oversight costs us an extra twenty minutes' walk when we reach the top.

After numerous stops for breath we do eventually reach the top and at one of the rest points a young walker passes us seemingly without noticing our presence.

"This is beginning to remind me of Wincobank," say I.
"The Carbrook Arms?" says Wen. "It was like we had ceased to exist."
"It's changed hands now," say I.
"Are they any better?"
"They can't be any worse."...

***

...Yes, yes... I see you.
I know.
You did not want to come again ... not yet... not when the tears still fall.
Not when rain bites you.
Not when the wind blows like winter's end.
But I called you.
You know my name... as I know yours.
It waits for you...it must be earned...as was mine.
Names matter, little sister.
Have I not said so?

***

..."There may be one consolation to coming this way," say I.
"And what's that?" says Wen.
"The last time I came this way there was an ice-cream van at the top of the hill."

We finally crest the rise and sure enough there she is. A somewhat dilapidated nineteen sixties type ice cream van is standing just about where I remembered it would be. That is the first thing I have been right about since we set off on this excursion and I would be misleading people if I did not admit that I for one could 'murder' for an ice cream after our more-arduous-than-it-needed-to be climb. As we draw nearer to the ice cream van, though, I start to become a little apprehensive. It is one thing to be driving a nineteen sixties ice cream van but it is quite another for the van to be still entrenched there, which to all intents and purposes appears to be the case. There is a faded, hand written price board in the window precariously perched behind ice cream adverts long since made indecipherable by the sun. The ice cream man turns out to be a woman, an old woman who stands arthritically, lumbers over to the window and beams us both a toothless smile. "You're the first people to come up that hill in three months," she cackles and fixes me with a piercing glare. I cannot help wondering whether she has been here for the whole of that time... waiting for us.

"We lost our way in the wood," say I, feeling some kind of response is in order however inadequate.
"What'll you two lovelies be having then?" says the ice cream woman straightening her back with a crack.
"We'll have two Ninety-Nines please," say I.

The ice cream woman turns to reach into the fridge and there is an almighty bang in the van. She immediately turns and asks, "Did you see that?"

"No," say I.
"What was it?"
"I didn't see anything... I heard it."
"Didn't you see it?"
"Didn't I see what?" say I.
"It was just the price board," says Wen picking it up off the counter and re-positioning it.
The ice cream woman starts to cackle again and points at Wen, "That's a lovely top, my pretty," and then to me. "Juice on your iced creams?"
"What have you got?"
"There's Raspberry, Strawberry or Chocolate."
"Chocolate please," say I.
"Now, you don't want chocolate."

"Why don't I want chocolate?"

"You don't want chocolate because it will spoil the taste of the ice cream."

"What would you recommend?"

"Have whatever you like love."

"Raspberry?" say I hoping against hope that I have made an acceptable choice.

"Raspberry it is."

I notice with some relief that the prices are not nineteen sixties prices.

Wen and I move away from the ice cream van towards the moor demolishing our ice creams.

"It was a black bird," says Wen quietly.

"What was?" say I.

"In the van," says Wen.

"There was a black bird in the ice cream van?" say I.

"That's what caused the noise," says Wen.

"A black bird flew inside the ice cream van?"

"Well it was black and it appeared to have wings and yes, it was definitely inside the van."

"Okay," say I and although it is the only thing I have got right so far today I am beginning to wish that I had been wrong about the ice cream van after all...

\*\*\*

...Do they hear me? The guardians who walk at your side?

Does my voice reach their soul as it does yours?

No, little one. I am dead to them: a mere dream. A memory whispered in the night. No more.

But for you...I have waited.

Do you ask why?

Think... feel... feel me...

Ah yes... you begin to see... as I saw.

I dreamed your becoming....

\*\*\*

..."There should be a gate out onto the moor."

Wen stops in front of a gate onto the moor attached to which there just happens to be a picture of an Ibis.

"I still think that's a Curlew," say I.
"It may well be," says Wen pensively, "but that doesn't preclude our other bird from Hordron's Edge being an Ibis."
"Thoth in Egyptian is 'duty' you know, or at least the word that became our duty."
"Djehuty!"
"It relates to the concept of dealing with what is due to you."
"In some of the Pyramid Texts Thoth is described as the brother of Osiris and Set... and he often sides with Set against Osiris..."

\*\*\*

...They gave me themselves... shared that gift... soul to soul.
A child... an empty vessel filled with the wisdom of the many... bittersweet liquor of loss and a last gift.
I carried them with me through the long night across the heather.
I sought shelter with the Raven.
Their wings brought me here.
Guarded... Secret... Safe...
I held their gift through the long years and never spoke it.
But I was waiting, always waiting...

\*\*\*

..."But that's not the right gate anyway there should be some steps in the wall alongside."

We move further down the hill and then we see it just as described: a gate with alongside in the wall protruding stones that serve as steps. This is far more of a relief than it should be but I was beginning to entertain the notion that I had dreamed the whole thing, or maybe imagined it.

"This is the baby," say I and start to clamber up the steps to get a better look out over the moor.

The moor is covered in bracken which means we will not be able to see the stone circle anyway. I am beginning to lose count of the disappointments.

"We could try and find Hob Hurst's House," says Wen contemplating the map, "it's not far."...

***

...*They did not die.*
I waited for the one who would come.
The one who would carry them, carry their wisdom back out into the world.
I waited until my years were a burden.
I waited until the weariness took my bones.
I waited.
And none came...

***

...It is at this point that the Wellington boots become an issue.

The book we are using these days as our preliminary guide is a good one. It has splendid descriptive passage of most of our sites and some rather lovely line drawings too. It is also obvious from the text that the author is more than sympathetic to his subject and he has a real empathy and feeling for the landscape and the sacredness of the sites that he has set out to describe. The maps however are mere sketches and Wen's cheerful, 'It's not far' turns out to be, 'a hell of a long way, actually,' and although the skies are leaden it is not cold and walking uphill through bracken... well you can imagine.

There is one thing though.

Every time we see a sign for Hob Hurst we also see a sign for Robin Hood...

***

...I stand and walk away, up towards the cairn, tears streaming. My companions watch me go, leaving me to my grief. That image has haunted me. Flame in her hand, love in her eyes spilling as tears on the cheeks of a child...she plunges the brand into the tinder and the flames take them. They *burn*...

Ah little one, *they* did not burn. Only bodies were consumed by flame as mine was consumed by time.
They did not die. Still I waited in the old places... at the edge of vision... I carried them still.
And then came one who walked the heart of the land, who felt its breath in the yearning of her soul. One who saw through the shroud of time and heard the cry of children in the fires. One who knew the searing and the tears and carried the mark of their branding.
Empty... an empty vessel, forged to be filled.
They did not die... I carry them still.

Don is beside me, I turn to his shoulder...
He is silent, but always there when the tears come.
The rain comes too... driving hard in the bitter, unseasonable chill. It always rains at the cairn. We should go back to the car before we are soaked. I set off in the other direction, following the calling voice... the cackle of an old woman on the wind...towards the house place.
I follow the path... now a stream... my slippers worse than useless. I must be mad. We walk into the storm, excoriated by the rain.
I dare not look at Don.
I look at my feet, one in front of the other, finding the path...

***

...Hob Hurst's House turns out to be something of a little beauty and as with most of these at first glance, perhaps, macabre sites, it has a lovely, reassuring feel to it but again it will be necessary to return for a proper assessment of its true scope when the foliage as died down.

I am sort of blaming myself for that one.

I should have known that we would not be able to see anything at this time of year and I particularly wanted Wen to get a sense of the necropolis as we walked the moor.

These places are always vast and they are always high...

***

...Between the mounds of the necropolis... guardians of the flight of vision...my own guardians following.
I hope.
Perhaps they have had the sense to return to the car... I, however, must go on. Mud squelches between my toes, my shoes carry only misery.
She walked this way... barefoot...
It was only in the winter of the year and in the winter of life that she accepted the fur boots her Guardian made for her.
Years and years... serving the chieftains, serving the people... yet for herself only the silent companionship of a love unspoken.
A silent grief of waiting...

***

...We are starting to lose height now and I can see the edge of the woods which means the monument will not be far, of that I can be certain.

...Certainty? My mind almost gags on the concept. There is nothing certain in memory. There is nothing certain in life. There is only the thin veneer of confidence with which we paint our experiences and then stand back, proudly, in order to look upon them with something akin to... certainty.

The path begins to fork and my mind groans again under the weight of the years. I have no recollection of which path we took so we follow the path around to the right... and end up at a lake.

"This is not the way we came."

The fact is there are gaps in memory. Huge yawning gaps which we are only too happy to forget because in our mind we do not actually travel. We flit like fleas. We jump and skip from one major incident or image to the next and we imagine they are all linked by a line. By the straight line of time which knows no forks or turnings or variance.

There is, though, another signpost for Robin Hood.

So we follow that...

\*\*\*

...We reach the house-place. My eyes see only the encircling wall of stones, a few courses high... standing stones in the walls... even here she did not escape the Seeing... Her eyes join mine and I see the angled roof of thatch... the low opening covered with hide.

A fire burns within and I enter.
By the door a rough cot covered with fur... On the far side an alcove, draped in hides to keep out the draught, piled with furs... a necklace of seashells, incongruous on the moor, lies beside the bed. Beneath it, I know, is the stone cyst where she placed their ashes. The last of the embers glow softly on the hearth.
The remains of a meal discarded.
It is warm, homely.
They were here not so long ago...

\*\*\*

..."This monument..." says Wen as we clear an opening in the trees.
"Have you found it?"
"I've found something!"

The monument turns out to be a four cornered Hunting Tower.
It is a huge thing. I mean, massive. This is definitely the place though; I remember the steps and the drooping chains, and the cannons. I ought really to have recalled the cannons. How could my mind have erased the Hunting

Tower and replaced it with a monument?

That is how the memory works.

If it encounters a gap it cannot fill it searches the archives and fills it with something it *has* got. It is not completely dishonest. It shrunk from actually putting my cenotaph where the Hunting Tower should be, but it got to the cenotaph from the drooping chains common to both and it knew the structure had height.

So it improvised and called it a monument or maybe that was me.

"I don't hold out much hope for our lost stone," say I looking up at the Hunting Tower.

Wen chuckles, "C'mon, you never know."

We have not gone far when we see yet another sign for Robin Hood.

And then it hits me... like a silver bullet...

"What if Robin Hood is the name of a stone?"

*** 

...There is no death, little sister.

We did not die.

We have waited for one to come.

I am the mead to fill the vessel...

You know my name...

And it is Knowledge.

*** 

..."I have never before been so passive in public," says Ben.

We are breakfasting in a little cafe in Ilkley and Ben is still glowing from the aftermath of our second workshop under The Silent Eye banner. More specifically he is referring to the outdoor ritual which Wen and I put together and more specifically still he is referring to his role in the ritual as Osiris.

To give the great man his due he did play the part exceedingly well.

In fact, it was a 'perfect' performance.

'The rapture' Wen calls it and insists that it is dangerous to stay too high too long especially when one has to operate in the now of the earth sphere.

'Time for another diagram,' I almost hear her say.

"What's this," says Ben, "Ah I was wondering when you were going to hit me with another one of these. I think I am starting to detect a little method in your infinite madness."

"You'll like this one," says Wen. "It's druidic."

"Ah yes, the druids," says Ben and rolls his eyes mysteriously. "I have been getting to know a little of their thought recently."

"This should be a cinch for you then," says Wen and winks at me in her now customary way.

"Good grief," says Ben, "it looks like the symbol from our aircraft during the second world war."

"That's precisely what it is," say I, "'Winnie' may not have been black but he *was* a druid."

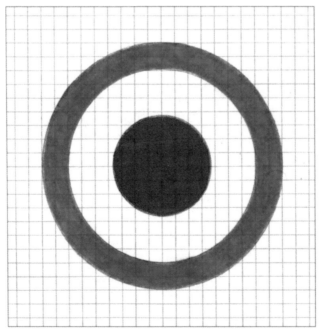

Figure 10 – '*The Lodestone.*'

"Churchill? Was he really? I had no idea it had come down so far."

"Oh yes, but Churchill was a 'renaissance druid', obviously," say I.

"Quite," says Ben, "but what does it all mean?"

"The central circle is the core of the earth, the red inner sun, which is molten stone. The blue band is the sky which can also be regarded as an emanation from the core, that's why it's blue when lit: essence of rock or stone. The white, though it pains me to say it, is the Awen, the place of inspiration where we, because we are blessed, have our being. We could live in a perpetual state of inspiration if we would only open up and get out of the way."

"So why does the stone sing for the king?"

"The king is the sun and the song comes from the birds in the sky."

"Do you see it?" says Wen.

"I see it," says Ben.

"Beautiful isn't it?" says Wen.

"I could never have imagined," says Ben in something of a whisper and then he asks as if from nowhere, "Did you know that a little 'i' is the sun at the top of a column?"

"Or that a capital 'I' links the heavenly and earthly realms," smiles Wen.

And after a long pause, Ben frowns, "But surely this is the fourth treasure, what happened to the third?"

Wen and I burst into laughter, and Ben joins us though I am not sure he remembers quite why.

'With them the Lode-Stone:
Beneath the tread of Albion's kings… it sings.'

\*\*\*

# Chapter Four:
## *Dark Ages*

"...Before there was anger, before there was tumult, before there was strife, before there was conflict the first company of the justified were born, before the Eye of Horus was plucked out..." – *The Royal Myth of Egypt.*

Figure 11 – *Sacred Yew*

"Don't you think it's odd," says Wen, "Osiris ends up in a pillar hewn from a tree, Odin hangs from a tree to gain sacred knowledge and Christ dies on a cross cut from a tree?"

"Well it's quite clearly the same story if that's what you mean," say I.

"You know Don," says Wen almost appreciatively, "only you could have used the phrase 'quite clearly' in that sentence."

"There's also the Merlin of course who falls from a height into a tree and seeing as though you appear to be going all historical on me these days, we might as well throw into the mix as well the Black Boy who hid in a tree before escaping to France."

"People do hide in trees though," says Wen.

"Children hide in trees all the time," say I, "but when a 'once and future' king hides in a tree it probably alludes to something a little bit more fundamental than a game of hide-and seek."

"To what does it allude though?" says Wen.

"Do you want my personal, probably improvable, opinion upon this matter or something more acceptable to the mainstream?"

"And since when have I ever wanted anything remotely acceptable to the mainstream?"

"I think they're all Green Men."

"Which isn't saying very much at all, Donald Sams, seeing as though no one has really satisfactorily explained what the Green Men, which pepper our churches in veritable abundance, allude to either?"

"The Green Man is the anthropomorphic representation of a tree spirit."

"Blood and sand," says Wen, "that's so mind numbingly obvious I'm surprised the question was ever posed. How did we miss that one?"

"We lose sight of these things from time to time."

"Somewhat ironic then, isn't it, that our mass information age could be regarded as the darkest, darkest time of all."

"Not in the slightest, that's usually the way it works."

\*\*\*

...As you can well imagine Ned, Wen and I are utterly saturated when we finally come off the Big Moor surrounding Barbrook One and as it is already quite late we really have only one option remaining to us. Ned graciously offers to foot the bill or the check as he calls it for dinner as a thank you for our efforts in guiding him through the weekend even though, strictly speaking we still have half a day on the morrow to fill. Wen already has plans for that one, looking on it as an opportunity for us to finally get to see the Anglican Cathedral of the city. Another look at the Catholic Cathedral too would not be unwelcome if only to drool over the wooden reliefs depicting the Stations of the Cross.

It is a peculiarity of the Catholic Faith to dwell on the final moments of Christ's human life in this way and I had always supposed that it represented a part of the Spiritual Exercises which were introduced by the Jesuits. One has to wonder about this bunch. They were all over the Enneagram when it first gained currency in the West and it is hard not to conclude that they have a good grasp of what it means to be human and possibly also what it means to be divine.

Why should it be deemed salutary to contemplate what to all intents and purposes is a Roman form of torture and execution? Well, if you have ever wondered about that I can only recommend a perambulation along the galleries of the Mary and All Saints Cathedral. The artist responsible for this work of genius has insisted that there are only three figures throughout. And that is immediately interesting looking at these things as I now do from an esoteric point of view. Wen and I first did the tour when we were working on the Green Fire Chapter of 'Giant's Dance' and but for that fact I may not have made the connection between the three deaths of the Merlin figure and the three falls of the Christ figure on his way to Calvary. Then there are the supplementary figures, one of them called Simon, who helps after the third fall and one of them hooded. I am assuming the hooded figure is the early introduction of our friend Joseph and one really has to wonder why this figure is always depicted in this way. Finally there is the Veronica who surely cannot be better named and cannot give any clearer clues as to what this process is really all about. So there you have it, the meaning of life in thirteen, fourteen or fifteen easy to comprehend stages...or not, as the case may be.

And right next to the final stage is a stained-glass window depicting Saint Michael slaying a green-faced devil.

Sometimes I despair.

\*\*\*

Despite, Morgana's insistence to the contrary, the church at Pilton *is* a St John the Baptist Church. Quite why she insists upon referring to it as a St Michael's I do not really know, perhaps because it is built on a hill with admittedly some rather suggestive prospects out over the old river valley below.

Be that as it may, the St John the Baptist churches have played a pretty significant part in our story to date and so the church at Pilton has a lot to live up to. It certainly does not disappoint but I *do* start to wonder whether the church at Pilton has always been a St John the Baptist church. There are a number of reasons for this, quite apart from Morgana's curious insistence. St John the Baptist churches generally tend to emphasise the figure of the Baptist over and above the figure of the Christ. This may sound odd in a Christian church but it is a fact. There may be no particular political point being made in this respect either but it is a fact nonetheless. The font for example, and by extension the rite of baptism, usually figures to a greater extent in these churches than in other churches and we have in our explorations come across St John the Baptist churches which have structurally celebrated this aspect of the church rite to a quite spectacular degree. The iconography too in these churches oft times dwells specifically upon the life of the Baptist rather than on the life of the Christ. In one of our early St John the Baptist churches in Buckinghamshire for example we found a huge wall mural painted in sepia tints depicting a scene which we at first, perhaps quite naturally, assumed to be the Sermon on the Mount but which, upon closer inspection, turned out to be the Baptist preaching to the multitudes. I could go on but I will not. Suffice it to say that the St John the Baptist church at Pilton is different. Quite markedly so for it is to all intents and purposes a normal church like any other and if anything it goes out of its way to celebrate the life of Christ to a perhaps greater extent than normal. The only stained glass in there for example depicts scenes from his life, however even in this there is something a little odd. Something we have not seen before but something that we both spotted almost immediately.

There is a transfiguration window at the west end of the church which casts its spectacularly coloured light over the baptismal font.

"What did the information board say?" says Wen.

"It says," say I, "'... 'Here, he built on the side of the hill above the harbour, where probably he baptised his first converts.'"

"Who did?" says Wen.

"Why, Joseph of Arimathea of course," say I.

"But of course," says Wen.

***

...After an all too brief sojourn in the Anglican Cathedral which was also a lot more impressive than I was expecting and after an impromptu cream tea to avoid the inevitable downpour on the way to the station we finally wave goodbye to Ned.

Wen has given him an exhaustive list of places to visit in Glastonbury which is Ned's next port of call, aside from the obvious, and on the top of that list of course are the St John the Baptist Churches of Glastonbury and Pilton.

Ned it turns out has something for us too, "Check out the cave at the back of the '...Drop' he whispers enigmatically upon leaving, "It may hold something of interest."

So Ned runs off happily into bright sunshine and a future that none of us really expected nor would have wished for despite all the clues being there....

***

..."I had read about the Joseph of Arimathea thing a long time before coming here," I muse, "and I suppose like many others I took it with a pinch of salt but being here, well it does feel special, and it is very easy to see it, almost even more difficult not to see it, actually, which of course makes the story all the more believable."

"It would make it far simpler though if Joseph *had* come over with the eleven disciples of Christ which as we know, he didn't."

"So where *did* they go?"

"Nobody really knows where they went."

"Isn't it in The Book?"

"The Book as you so quaintly put it only really deals with Peter and Paul."

"Would that be Paul who wasn't even a disciple?"

"I know... there are a lot of imponderables in the construction of the 'testament'.

"And isn't that in itself a little odd?"

"It could certainly be construed that way, especially as the Gospels are purportedly eye witness accounts of the disciples which bear their name."

"There is a Simon though isn't there, he's depicted in one of the windows in Glastonbury's St John the Baptist Church."

"Simon Zelotes?"

"That's the fellow. Presumably he is avowedly not the Simon who followed Christ even though to be zealous could be interpreted as to be disciplined in one and the self-same way."

"You are correct. He is avowedly not the same Simon because the Simon that followed Christ was Simon Peter ergo he was in actual fact Peter."

"Wait a minute, wait a minute!"

Wen pauses and looks at me expectantly.

"Didn't Peter aka Simon deny the Christ?"

"He did, as most people are aware. He famously denied the Christ three times on the night of his arrest around a fire just before the break of day."

"Maybe this is what the Zelotes tag is emphasising. Maybe the Simon Peter who denied Christ was known forever after as Simon the Denier or some such derogatory appellation."

"It's possible," says Wen somewhat disinterestedly, "there may even have been two Simons' from the off necessitating the initial name change."

"And there's always Simon of Cyrene, he was there or thereabouts at the end and could easily have been invited along for services rendered."

"The window could also very easily be making the very pertinent political point that the Simon who came here was true to the cause. But this does now start to sound like the beginnings of another wild and woollier than thou theory."

So I change tack.

"Did they all carry staffs?"

"Really Don, how should I know, and why would that make a difference anyway."

Figure 12 – '*Saint or Hero?*'

"Well, we know what Joseph did with *his* staff but what if that was all part of the 'mission' or whatever it is you'd want to call it: what if all twelve of them carried a staff and planted it where they decided to settle and what if like Joseph's thorn all the staffs took root, grew and blossomed."

"In which case there would be more than one Holy Thorn in the precincts of Glastonbury."

"Not necessarily: they wouldn't all have to be thorns, in fact it would be a little strange if any of the other staffs *were* from thorns."

"I'm not sure I follow."

"Joseph's tree was only a thorn because of the crown..."

\*\*\*

"So what's with this Grateful Dead thing anyway?" says Wen.

"The Grateful Dead is a particular type of folk tale in which the protagonist meets with and converses with dead people, usually though not always on the night of All Hallows Eve."

"So, they're ghost stories?"

"If you like I suppose, although personally speaking I'd like to think there is a little bit more to them than that."

"In what way?" says Wen her interest piqued for very obvious reasons.

"Well I don't think they are supposed to frighten people like your average ghost story, nor indeed to warn them off the investigation of such things. As the title may indicate the stories usually involve truck with the dead in a positive way such that the protagonist receives a boon for helping them out or such like."

"Can you give me an example?"

"Let's see now... well one of the first stories to be dealt with is a young man and his grandfather, who has been hanged..."

"Ah, I can see the link with Devil's-Drop already," says Wen.

"So the game young lad trips out to the gallows, and the ghost of his grandfather climbs down off the scaffold and asks him for a drink of water which the young lad duly fetches and from that time on his grandfather's ghost, being so grateful for the parching of his thirst, is always on hand to help him out of any sticky situations that he might find himself in."

"The young lad in fact now has supernatural aid!"

"That's another way of looking at it I suppose but that is a very basic type of the tale. The variants are many and diverse and perhaps the most interesting is one of the more involved tales in which something of a reversal takes place."

"Oh really, in what way is a reversal effected?"

"Well the young lad is promised supernatural help in securing a bride on the proviso that upon having secured her he allows her to spend half the year with the dead. It's an interesting twist and it could almost be the missing prequel to the infamous myth of Persephone. Always assuming there is a missing prequel of course."

"Yes, yes I see," says Wen somewhat pensively.

Wen's pensive mood becomes pervasive and I pick up a little of what she is thinking.

It is true. It does not always feel like what *we* do has too many material boons or benefits.

Maybe we are doing it wrong?

***

How long have I shrunk from an attempt to describe this place?
How often have I found myself here?

...Always.

It is disturbing but as a construct it remains, and so, it is comforting also
...to my left is a familiar room filled with friends who shout and smile and raise their glasses as I enter.
Only the bar-man remains suspicious.
He has abused me on more than one occasion and often ignores me when I attempt to order drinks.
This room is L-shaped and I stand in the far right at the foot of the L. contemplating the door opposite and wondering whether I should seat myself upon one of the red-leather wall seats, along with the old man who beckons to me with an extended hand and a cheery countenance, or instead, leave without buying a drink.
The man sits at the far end of the L in the right hand corner and a little to one side of his right shoulder is a small window, plumb in the middle of the back wall. This is the only window in the room. The room is very smoky, very noisy and very dark.

As I consider my predicament, the old man seems to lose interest and turns his attentions upon his dead wife who is propped up alongside.

He talks to her as he re-arranges her clothes and tidies her appearance as if for meeting company. The drink before her is untouched and flat. When he has supped his own beer the old man will quickly finish his wife's and then buy another round. I have seen him do this on a number of occasions.

Nobody minds.

The scene saddens me and I grow depressed, wondering just how I came to be here.

I am struck by a thought...
'This man, the one who drinks with his dead wife; this man, whose smile expresses joy in decay: this man knows a lot more than he is telling.'

It is essential to hold onto this idea.

I enter through a wooden door, and it is like this...

To my left is the breakfast-bar and beyond and behind, to my left is the timber-frame of a half constructed partition wall. The unfinished wood is rough and splinters at a touch. The wall contains a window without glass.

It is difficult to describe what lies beyond the partition. It is spacious, certainly and when I move into it I trip over myself playing games, on the floor, with a girl whose name escapes me...

We crawl and scuffle and laugh and I look up ashamedly because a man stands in the doorway, moves towards us and strides resolutely over our heads.

There has been a party but the party is over now. Only the wreckage remains... bodies... bottles... and stains.
There will be no more partying now the stranger is here.
He runs his hand around the window-frame collecting splinters.
But this, I will never achieve and I never reach the partition wall from the

front like that.

It is always after the party.

I am leaving, escaping this place.

I come from inside, from the door over yonder which conceals stairs leading upwards... and beyond.

It is from this beyond that I have come.

Down from the behind and beyond, up from below.

No, I never walk like that from the front turning left.

I never turn left like that but move forwards, straight...

*** 

... "...And is there a record of any such tree plantings?" says Wen.

"Nope, but then there's no record of anything," say I.

"What, nothing at all?"

"Zilch! Joseph brings the grail, allegedly, gets given the hides of land, sets up his followers in situ and then we hear nothing more of them until our mutual friend from '...Ætheling...'"

"What, Good King Lucius?"

"The very same, who then, according to the account proceeds to in some way re-establish the whole process with works and buildings and such like."

"How long is the time gap?"

"...about two hundred years and the description of the intervening years are, shall we say, interesting..."

"Go on then, let's hear it..."

"'Saint Joseph's little circle of twelve disciples was kept going by anchorites – as one died another was appointed but in course of time a certain slackness seems to have come over them. William of Malmesbury tells us that the holy spot at length became a covert of wild beasts...'"

At which point neither Wen nor I can contain ourselves any longer and we both explode into paroxysms of laughter...

I need to explain that Wen has a 'thing' about 'Hairy Anchorites.'

"But go on... if you can..."

"Okay... I'll try, 'Then in the days of Good King Lucius came a revival, Llewrig Mawr, the Great Luminary... increased the Light that the first missionaries, the disciples of Christ, had brought...'"

"Ah, but Little Grub, correct me if I am wrong, but hasn't this text just stated that the first missionaries *were* the Disciples of Christ?"

"No correction, O Something Feral, but the statement could be nothing more than a generalisation?"

"Generalisation or not the time frame is also interesting."

"Pray tell how so, O Woolly One?"

"Why, two hundred years is about the time usually given for the period generally referred to in our, perhaps not quite as accurate as we would like to believe, historical records as... the Dark Ages!"

"Llewrig Mawr actually means The Great King of Light," says Wen quietly.

"Which sounds pretty much like the Christ himself to me," say I cheerfully...

And then I have a thought. It is an excessively hairy thought to be sure and I am not sure that even the redoubtable Wen will appreciate its scale and ramifications.

In all probability then, I reason, the thought does not belong to me but I keep it to myself anyway.

Which it could be argued might well be construed as theft of a sort.

"You're thinking something," says Wen, "I can tell." Then she raises her eyebrow which probably means that like it or not, want to or not, I am going to have to 'cough'...

"What if the 'hell' that Christ harrowed was Albion?"

*** 

...Before me is a room. Not the room with a breakfast bar.

This room begins were all other rooms end, without walls.

This room is long and friendly and filled with family. The lounge or tap-room of a public house with a round-bar in the corner...

To my right, by the open window stands the Old Man, his fingers bound by gold and mounted stone. His heavy coat is laden with regalia and the mantle of ages and is worn with casual grace. The lights of the machine before him follow his will and call forth fortunes in vast, raucous abundance.

He always gains in this way but now he must leave and motions for my attention. I stand before him as he lifts his mantle and places the heavy weight upon my shoulders. Apparelled thus, I feel like a gross child taking obscene strides towards an end which forever recedes and I can never catch the stage-coach which in all ways leaves without me...

I love though to be swift. Only by shedding this skin can I board the stage and again re-enter my room...

But all now has become, suddenly... noise, the babble of lively voices, and hubbub of warm conversation...

I approach his corner, walking the whole length of the room, thinking how best to draw him out, and, sitting down at his table, and leaning over conspiratorially; I whisper solemnly into his ear, "Within a story, hides the world." The old man grins and titters in glee, his face contorting, obnoxious and hideous as he cackles, rocking upon his haunches, slapping his knees. He eventually recovers and after wiping away his mirth with a cupped hand, like a mime, becomes deadly serious. He stares and slowly revolves his eye-balls white into his eye-lids. I laugh at this performance, uncertain and nervous, but as he persists, my laughter becomes silence...The Old Man's eyes revolve and he titters again and points, enjoying my amazement.

These games are played out for our mutual benefit...

I shake my head, smiling, and drink. He slaps his knees and nods furiously in encouragement, picks up his wife, still chuckling beneath his breath, heaves her over his shoulder and struggles from the room. I have been drinking from her glass, and now the bar is emptying. Tables lie strewn, upturned on the floor. Ash-trays have been spilled. Beer swills the clutter. There has been a party but the party is over now. There will be no more partying now that the Old Man has gone.

*** 

... "Next up Vee!" says Wen watching Ned's form recede.

"Next up, after Scort-Land, that is!"

"Don't let the Scots hear you say that," grins Wen. "It's a pity we couldn't have had them both here at the same time."

"There's always next year," say I.

"Where to now, then?" says Wen.

I can tell from her tone that she is keen to continue with the Quest as we playfully refer to the Work, but I for one am all for a somewhat more leisurely remainder of the day...and a little assimilation; where Wen is concerned the term Dragons and the phrase 'chasing them' are always closely aligned and never too far away.

Wen smiles in acquiescence, "Which pub did you have in mind?"

***

# Chapter Five:
## *Shadows of the Future...*

"The Living Monument: All the henge stones were thought to be alive, both individually and as the cells of a larger organism."

– The Avebury Cycle, Michael Dames.

Figure 13 – *'Death in the Green'...*

It may be because Wen cannot sleep too well....

...All this chasing around. Wen would happily spend all morning, afternoon and most of the evening driving here there and everywhere and then set about writing up the exploits of the day before retiring for what she calls sleep.

Upon leaving me on Tuesday she is driving up to Scotland for a couple of days and then driving all the way back down here on the Friday with Vee before picking me up and then setting off for Stockport for our Lodge Meeting after which... she is driving us back to mine.

On top of which she is also due to give a guided meditation at the meeting which when she left me on Tuesday she had not even begun to think about.

I, on the other hand, am always falling asleep.

"Why is that?" says Wen, "Why *are* you always falling asleep?"

"Because, my dearest Wendlebury, my dreams are more real than the reality I experience when I am awake..."

\*\*\*

## The Grey Chapel

*Breathe deeply, still your thoughts and prepare for a guided journey...*

You are standing on a green lawn, surrounded by a grove of trees that mask the surrounding countryside... gnarled oaks, yew and rowan you recognise, other trees you do not. There is a quality to the light and the clouds that make you feel that you are high upon a mountain perhaps or a hilltop, but the veil of green prevents you from seeing where you are.

The grass feels pleasantly warm to your bare feet and, looking down, you see that you are dressed in a plain, white robe.

The air is hushed; no sound except the breeze in the trees, an almost subliminal whispering, and the twitter of birds sheltering unseen in their branches.

Before you is a monumental building of silver grey stone. It appears to be circular in form with a square porch full of deep blue shadows. Similar porches can be glimpsed at either side, marking the quarters, but as you walk around the perimeter of the structure you see that there is only one entrance; the three other squares seem to be windowless chapels and, in fact, you see no windows at all. A domed roof covers the building, made of precisely shaped blocks of stone, yet light must enter somehow, for it streams through the shadows within, painting a white path on the ground at your feet.

There seems nowhere else to go, no pathway through the dense trees, nothing except this path of light to follow. Taking a deep breath you place your feet upon it and walk towards the porch.

The walls are perfectly smooth…undecorated and stark... The silence, however, is light and gentle and the feel of the place is one of both peace and power. Deepest blue shadows cluster around you as you walk between the walls of silver stone and as you enter the porch the silence becomes complete, broken only by the sounds of your life… your heart, your breath, the soft fall of your bare feet and the whisper of the soft fabric of your robe.

The light has faded, taking on the quality of starlight.

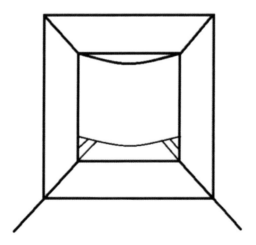

As you reach the end of the porch you see a curved corridor falling away to left and right, following the contour of the building, with shallow steps leading down either side like the rays of the sun.

In front of you there is a curved inner wall of pure white marble, seamless and polished to an almost mirror-like sheen that reflects your image in the dancing shadows.

There is nothing to tell you which way to go, so you call upon your knowledge and understanding, and choose to walk deosil, in the direction of the sun. Taking the path that leads to the left you descend the shallow steps to reach the main curve of the corridor.

The shadows are deeper here, the silence too. The curving path curtails vision; you can see only a little way ahead and behind as the way fades into shadow. The outer world seems a distant memory. Yet there is no fear... and soon the steps rise before you once more and you find yourself on a landing similar to the first, save that here there is no exit to the left, only one of the chapels you saw outside.

You enter the room.... It is square with a domed roof of its own. In the centre of the ceiling a circular void lets in a shaft of light that falls like a pillar to the ground, seeming too solid and tangible to be the light you know. It is too bright to see the sky above, yet you feel that a night has passed and a new day begun. Beyond the light you can see a figure against the far wall, white, shadowed blue against the silver stone. Is it a statue perhaps? You peer through the light and see that is a Child. You cannot see it clearly... the light is too bright and for some reason you fear to enter into it. Yet there is something about that Child that warms your heart, awakening a yearning within you to reach out and touch it, know it...

You rest in contemplation, trying to understand what it is that you see...

After a while you turn and as you reach the place between the steps you see that there is a barred gate in the curved inner wall before you. It seems to be made of some silver metal, closely wrought. You can barely see through the gaps... just enough to glimpse a white light within a central circle. There is no handle and the gate yields not to your touch.

You step away and continue the clockwise circumambulation, down another set of steps, along another shadowed stretch and up another rise of stairs to a third landing. You look, but here there is no gate in the curvature of the inner wall.

There is, however, another chapel and you enter inside.

Again the shaft of light bars your way, but this time there is something in the white light, some indefinable quality of a noon in high summer. Beyond the shaft another figure, marble white... you cannot see clearly... a warrior or a hunter, perhaps...you do not know what it is but there is something of courage and endurance about the stance...something you recognise. Instinctively you straighten your spine, drawing yourself up to match that example... somehow it reminds you of yourself, the stronger side that the world seldom sees.

Again you stand in contemplation of what this might mean, before turning back and continuing along the path, down another set of stairs, through the shadows and once more up to the fourth landing. You have begun to get a feel for the place and its shape speaks to you. You are lost in thought as you walk into the chapel.

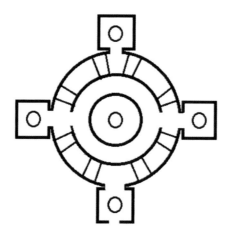

The shaft is of light, pure white, yet has the feeling of sunset. You sense, rather than see, the colour of blood on an unseen horizon and the figure on the wall speaks of death. Yet the building does not end here… it is a circle, without beginnings, whose path leads up and down, through shadow to light in an endless round. The figure seems to have suffered… is death a welcome release perhaps, or simply another step in the dance?

You consider these things without fear, feeling them in your own life echoing into the future.

Turning, you face the corridor and see another gate. This one stands open, yet the way is barred.

The figure is dressed in a simple white robe, identical to your own. His hands are folded on his breast and hidden in his sleeves, his head shaven, his eyes look into your own.

You feel naked before his gaze. There are no adornments, nothing to show his office, yet he exudes power. You feel you should kneel before such might, yet the memory of the warrior comes to you and you stand straight, holding yourself tall before him. His eyes are kind, radiating love and a gentle severity. You suddenly know the meaning of *awe*.

No words are spoken, yet his voice sounds in your being.

*You may not pass this way. Your time has not yet come.*

Beyond him you see the central circle, molten gold illuminated by the brilliance of the light that streams in from above.

*This is the place of the Cosmic Christ… the Christ as Magus, here at the navel of the worlds.*

He raises his hands and within them he holds a Cup. Light seems to stream into it. You think of the stories of the Grail Chapel and wonder… you think of the entrance to this place that somehow seems to echo the shape of the Cup. So, perhaps, does the shape of this Temple…and yet, there is more…

Threads of understanding begin to come together in your mind and heart as the Priest holds the Cup towards you with a smile.

*Whom does the Grail serve?*

You do not know if the thought is his or yours…or if there is a difference…You bend your head, covering his hands with yours, and, closing your eyes against its brilliance, you drink the liquid Light.…

When you open your eyes once more, both Priest and gate are gone.

There is now only the smooth curve of white marble before you and the silver path of light at your feet.

Turning, you continue back to the entrance and, taking a last look around, you follow the path back through the blue shadows of the porch… back into the glade where now the sun has set and the moon rides high and silver in the heavens, casting its pathway on the dew-damp grass.

You feel the cool wetness on your feet, and look up at the wheel of stars, closing your eyes and drinking in the silver light of life.

*Slowly you become aware once more of your body, feel the earth beneath your feet … and when you are ready, come back into the room, carrying with you the essence of your journey…*

*\*\*\**

…It is quite something to have Vee along to our meeting as a visiting dignitary although the news from Glastonbury is not good. Unfortunately, Ned did not get to any of our recommended haunts in the vicinity. In fact he barely got to the Tor before being called away urgently on family business.

I think back to our sojourn in the Anglican Cathedral. How I felt moved to ignite a light for loved ones passed which I had never done before at any of our previous church visits.

But if a shadow has been cast over our expedition it is a shadow mixed with light for the weather has taken a turn for the better and we head off down to Stockport in the brightest of bright sunshine.

We keep an eye open for our new pub which is apparently on the way and with what proves to be perfect synchronicity Vee makes the sign of the cross as we pass Devil's Drop.

Inevitably, given the amount of miles covered by Wen and Vee already today, we are a little late for the meeting but Ben waits until our arrival before commencing. He is as thrilled as we are to have Vee in attendance and the additional energy she both brings and facilitates certainly makes for an interesting gathering...

...As we head off into the night back to the Field of Sheaves after an exhilarating get together we are accompanied by an orange moon.

I think we all know to what it alludes although none of us voices our concerns despite having been asked to keep talking by Wen in order to help make sure she stays awake long enough to get us safely back.

There are some things which it is beyond the spoken word to convey.

***

...Wen, Ben and I have convened a meet up in Ilkley in order to reconnoitre the Moors with a view to 'doing something' up there and as might be supposed from such judiciously applied inverted commas this 'doing something' is not going to be quite your everyday run of the mill affair, not by any manner of means.

Quite what Ben has in mind will probably only properly materialise after we have taken a look at the terrain but from what Wen has already told me about his plans I have a very uneasy feeling about the whole thing.

Ostensibly the idea is to mark our new status as a Triad in some way, which is fair enough, but Ben seems to have taken it upon himself to assume the lead in this and my feelings of unease are somehow linked to this 'taking the lead'; not because I do not think that Ben has a perfect right to do this, because in some ways he clearly has, but because like it or not there are more than the three of us involved in the Triad and the intimations I am getting from this, for want of a better term, 'fourth' are not good, which to my mind at least is an indication that it, whatever it is, is not happy with the state of affairs as they currently stand..

Wen is of a similar mind to me on this but what can we do?

"There's not a lot we *can* do," says Wen, "except go with the flow."

***

...We are due to re-meet up with Vee at ten o clock the following morning and Wen has put together something of a hectic whistle-stop tour of the area. Bearing in mind that Vee is a little limited exertion wise we are probably going to have to concentrate on drivable views and churches which is in stark contrast to Ned's tour, so at least there will be some variation for us and we have more than enough to go at in both those areas.

Vee though has other ideas and when we do meet up we spend the first two hours of our 'whistle stop tour' sitting out in the sun conversing about, well everything under that sun really, but primarily about what it is perhaps best to refer to as the Work, and Vee's somewhat unexpected and unasked for introduction to it.

Vee is a consummate story teller and we could probably have spent longer out there but it would have been a pity to lose such a glorious day weather wise entirely to talk so we head off in search of ice cream oysters which we enjoy whilst looking out over the Lady-Bower beneath which, Wen assures me, is a submerged village. This reservoir, like many others, had been artificially created by flooding a previously inhabited valley, which sets me thinking... bearing in mind that submerged cities are something of a mythological mainstay I cannot help wondering what the village would look like now and whether or not it would be possible to get some shots of it...
This would though, no doubt, require a boat and a wet suit and a mask, not to

mention the flippers and oxygen cylinders. It would also presumably entail lessons in scuba diving and underwater photography which, all things considered, makes it a rather absurd thought to be having whilst eating an ice cream on a hot summer's day in May.

*** 

...Whatever our reservations it is not easy to be unhappy about an excursion on Ilkley Moor and I say this as something of a newcomer to the place. Wen, who pretty much grew up here is positively ecstatic so while Ben busies himself drawing up his plans for our ritual sojourn here at the turn of the year, Wen and I amuse ourselves with the wildlife and the terrain, which of course does not disappoint. How could it?

Ben appears to be basing his ideas around a four-fold plan with specific reference to the elements. A sound enough basis for sure and being outside with the elements will probably give an added frisson to the work we have already done with them. The sites he has picked out, with Wen's help, are all eminently fit for purpose and my only real qualm perhaps is that there seems to be a goodly amount of walking involved in a relatively short space of time which Ben is keen to make even more arduous by loading us up with, well we are not quite sure what yet... except that Ben assures us that it will be 'intelligent'. Well really, could anyone ever accuse Ben of being unintelligent? From what Wen later tells me this is a much toned down version of what was originally conceived, with all manner of bodily deprivations planned for the three of us. This, to my mind at least, is slightly worrying and whilst I accept that these things have to be earned there are ways and means of earning them quite adequately enough without resorting to such extremes...

"We will have to give it a name," says Wen.
"We will have to give what a name?" say I.
"Our fourth," says Wen.
"Let's for arguments sake call it 'Dimension'," say I.

"It is to embody the struggle to raise ourselves from the earth," says Ben when asked about the loads we shall be carrying on our long, long walk out over the moor.

***

...Our next port of call with Vee is at the Strines Inn which quite apart from the fact that it is licensed to sell alcoholic beverages has two things going for it; the rather splendid views out over the Derbyshire landscape and the birds in the back garden. Of course the birds in the back garden do not always stay in the back garden which means that one can be happily supping ones Special Stout in the beer garden out front as a peacock struts past your table. This I imagine can be quite disconcerting to those poor souls who do not know about the birds in the back garden.

Wen and I though are old hands at this drinking with the birds' malarkey and it does not faze us one little bit although I have to own that I do find birds of all persuasion incredibly fascinating. They, even more than other creatures, perhaps, appear to my untrained eye to inhabit an entirely different realm to the rest of us, even the flightless ones which, strictly speaking, peacocks are not of course.

It is almost as if we are seeing only their shadow forms here in this world and that in another dimension somewhere are indestructible forms of the same creatures even more graceful... and strange... and wonderful.

As if to prove Vee's point about them being able to fly up into trees, which I for one am not wholly sure about, the loudest of the peacocks and the one continuously making the most noise appears to be doing so from branches halfway up a tree.

We go in search of the inevitable blog-shot for Wen and find that his perch is being guarded by a silent yet watchful and not-to-be-messed-with gaggle of geese.

A veritable king surrounded by his courtiers no less.

Perhaps it is Vee who is somehow depositing these alien ideas in my head. She also seems to be expert at extracting confessions like the one I feel compelled to admit over lunch.

"I had a bit of a 'Gothic Phase' myself. Death Maidens we used to call them."

\*\*\*

...On our way back from the moor we drive through some of Wen's old haunts. In particular we pass her Grandfather's house. As we do so there just so happens to be a chap in the garden smoking a cigarette and after he has flashed past Wen regrets not having stopped and asked him if the Isis which her Grandfather painted is still in situ over the stairwell.

"We can always go back," say I.
"We can never go back, says Wen.

It *is* a little like already being dead. One of the things I noticed quite early on when writing is that those things that *are* put down on paper, invariably, disappear. Even the people who could have verified their existence, sometimes, are no longer around, and even if they are they do not always remember. Caz, for example, has no recollection of the wild and unexpected appearance of the Isle of Man 'bang smack' in the middle of a Fleetwood Hotel window even though she was there and whilst in all probability not actually sitting next to me she could not have been too far away. Dad though does recall a number of similar experiences of his own which is something of a relief. We must thank heaven for the old in spirit; one never knows when one is going to need them. Am I to go in search of Ali and Sal and demand a photograph of a stone which may or may not have once been known as Robin Hood and which they probably never even had printed? Should I root out Bill Bell-Shank for confirmation of the shop that sold Lager & Lime as well as Cider flavour ice lollies but which now just looks like, and doubtless is, someone's home? It is a little disconcerting to have the things one has set ones store by so arbitrarily dismantled in such a way.

The human soul it seems is intrinsically tied up with impermanence.

\*\*\*

...Next up for Vee is The Old Horns Inn in High Bradfield, and we already appear to be developing a theme.

"Pubs with Great Views," says Wen.

"With the added bonus that this one also has a church," say I.

"When we brought Ned here," says Wen, "he shook his head forlornly, buried it in his hands and declared, 'I hate this, I so hate this!'"

"That sounds like Ned," laughs Vee.

The thing is... this is the first time we have been to High Bradfield in good weather. It does not affect the view of course but it does allow us more time to enjoy it, and enjoy it we do, principally whilst sitting on a grave slab in the church yard of St Nicholas' surrounded by inquisitive sheep and not so inquisitive locals. "He keeps eating sheep poo," says one young girl as she drags her reluctant dog from between the uprights. Vee finds a number of stones in the yard on which are engraved her maiden name.

If one *were* to repatriate I can think of worse places to live.

We eventually repair to the inside of the church.

Going around churches with different people is curious.

One sees different things.

Almost like one is seeing through their eyes.

Figure 14 – '*Parched Sun...*'

"A pity we didn't clock the Green Man when Ned was here," says Wen.

"It's more than a pity," says Vee. "He would have loved that."

"I can always send him a snap," says Wen.

When we finally make it to the Old Horns Inn the day is getting on somewhat and the rush for dinner is well underway.

So we elect to sit outside and quite by chance find ourselves at the 'Little Grub' table and feeling somewhat duty bound to relate the story to Vee...

"You two are having far too much fun with this," she concludes.

*** 

William Bell-Shank was Madeline's very first boyfriend.

I remember watching them together in the Park-Keeper's Paddock of Clayton Cemetery, in amongst the garden tools, alongside the Greenhouse, with the hoes and spades, the pitch-fork, and the pick-axe...

...Sara and Samantha have dressed for the occasion...

Samantha is in black, horsing about with a broom, careering up and down one side of the embankment which tunnels Cromwell Road before the railway bridge... Sara, accompanies her in a hooded white sheet, which gusts and flaps wildly as she runs, displaying her thighs, 'whooping' and 'wooing', and cackling loudly...

Bill and I have finally thrown off the newly shorn sheepishness of our new haircuts as we follow, laughing, excited...

... Madeline looks especially lovely tonight. The clear sky has accentuated her beauty by heightening her vague intransigence. The graveyard is one of the few places in which something approaching natural light is allowed to reign in White-Lake and natural light possesses the sort of affinity with Madeline's features which most sculptors and photographers can only dream about.

She is wearing neat, flimsy clothes which seem to do no more than veil her presence. I lean upon the paddock wall, unnoticed while she and Bill manoeuvre themselves apart from the others and slink to a quiet corner unobserved...

Madeline kisses tentatively and then seems a trifle disappointed as they part from each other and Bill moves away...

... But now she is looking directly at me, which I'm sure she never actually did...

And I am suddenly thirteen years old again and struggling to keep up with the brisk strides which Bill Bell-Shank is taking as he navigates the busy crowd of tourists before the shop fronts of White-Lake promenade. He halts momentarily to indicate our destination and my gaze follows his to the brightly coloured trellis above our head.

...'Mad Maud and Crazy Ken's Fancy Goods. '...

We are inside the shop and Bill has finally halted at the far end of one of the displays. He is toying with a small gold coloured cylinder of lipstick. He removes the lid and after ascertaining that he has my attention he slowly begins to twist the end of the cylinder. As the lipstick emerges to take the form of an erect penis, Bill's body starts to shake with laughter and at the sight of my bemused features he points to the display card which reads...

"LIPDICK ' - £ 2.00 a stick."

"Alright, alright, you've had your fun now clear off out of it..."

It is Crazy Ken, and Bill and I are back outside on the promenade bent double with laughter as we lurch away towards the Pier front where our bicycles rest together, locked to the promenade rail...

When I reach my bike it is now resting against red brick and loose mortar and Bill and I are about to sound the bell as we enter the corner shop on Grim Street, half-way home...

... We buy Larger &Lime and Cider flavoured ice lollies because it makes us feel like we are almost grown up and from here on in until we reach Bees-Grove the trick is to ride without having recourse to our handle bars.

We cruise down Wellington Road where Bill once sprayed rain-water from a puddle onto a family group of passers-by, and take a wide, wide arc, impossible if the grizzly sound of engine noise is heard, drifting around the tight corner, to swing smoothly onto North Minster Drive, a slight incline, but still manageable without a head-wind, before finally turning right onto Murky Depths Road and hurtling down, down towards the traffic of Cromwell Road and across that without stopping, without even looking... if we are extremely lucky... to coast triumphantly onto the dog-leg of Bees-Grove Road...

... Back in Clayton Cemetery, on the far side of the Greenhouse, Samantha is pushing Sara in the Park-Keeper's Wheel-barrow... tilting the barrow from side to side as she goes, with Sara bouncing and screaming and yelping as the barrow lurches noisily over the bumpy ground until Samantha finally laughs out loud in triumph as the wheel thuds against rock and pitches Sara, face first into the Park-Keeper's compost heap.

Figure 15 – 'Whom does the Grail serve?'

# Chapter Six:
## *...In a present no longer past.*

"Father, into thy hands I commend my Spirit."

- *Luke 23:44-46*

Figure 16 – *'Womb-Stone.'*

"In what sense are the stones alive?" says Wen.

"Well the folk records usually list three," say I.

"That's a good start," says Wen. "What are they?"

"The stones are often said to dance..."

"The Giant's Dance..."

"...Quite. But did you notice the last time we were in Morgy's office..."

"...I know," says Wen, "the Glastonbury landscape figures are also known as Giant's... the same poster was in the 'King Arthur.'"

"...The stones are said to turn..."

"To turn," says Wen. "Turn about, turn around, or turn inside out, what?"

"All three probably...Starts to sound like another dance doesn't it..."

"Well folk doubtless did dance through the stones, the males one way, females the other criss-crossing their energies..."

"...but I think the dancing and the turning could also be synonymous and refer to the mind meld..."

"The Wayland's effect..."

"Which as we know is 'a smiting', another transfer of energy...and the stones are said to move to and from bodies of water."

"Moving water?" says Wen.

"Rivers and streams usually, sometimes ponds or wells."

"The depths of time, the sources of life," hazards Wen.

"Possibly... and water tempers steel..."

"...There are a lot of circles named for nine..."

"The water here though is probably a telluric flow of earth energy."

"Maidens... Ladies..."

"There really should be a Crones circle too then, somewhere..."

"It might be interesting experimenting with a Nine's circle although of course the names don't always match the number of stones. Hordron's being a classic case in point...."

"You could bring some red and blue cord..."

"Really?" says Wen brightening.

"I think the stones are living monuments of dream if they are living monuments of anything..."

"You think that it is in our dreams that they live?"

"I'd say that was more than admirably put, Little Grub."

"Why, Something Feral, you are *too* kind."

## MANSIONS OF THE SOUL...

### The First Night: ...

### Draumas Mucgwyrt (A Dream of Mugwort)

The speared soul flies free, drawn across the land, searching, dripping pain like blood upon the earth, angry at its own judgement.

No higher gift than sacrifice, no greater folly than to seek to buy the Light for others with a life bound to the Tree.

Below the neat fields of his people; the wide plains and deep forests, sleeping, unaware of his passage, but he is drawn onwards.

He pays the price and seeks the gift.

Carved in wood, the rune blazes before the single eye of vision.

Tall stems bend in the breeze, grey flowers in a grey world.

Souls feed from the leaves like butterflies, drawing an essence that the plant cannot touch within itself but for which it yearns.

The spirit of the herb lifts its face to the sun and hides its regal heart in silver strands held by the dragon from whose scales it sprang.

He calls; it comes to his hand and becomes itself within him.

Roots, fine as spiders silk, spread through his flesh, branching, speaking, singing away anger and leaving only wisdom.

### The Second Night...

### Draumas Fille (A Dream of Thyme)

He reaches within to feel the need… and reaches far.

Past care, beyond service, to the broken core; a child besmirched, mired by a victim's wound, crying for a love that needs its need.

The rune flames in his heart.

Perfume draws him; its source crushed underfoot, insignificant, unnoticed, yet puissant in potential.

The purple of a livid bruise and the softness of sunset flowers in the grass, tumbling over stones, finding the smallest crevice in which to cling to life; fingers in the heart of stone.

The scent is clean, pungent, driving out the miasma of fear that lingers, banishing the septic cry that wails silently on the wind.

In its place is the scent of honeyed days and summer laughter.

A child plays; flaxen hair tousled by the breath of the sun, he watches his reflection in the stream, knowing he is not alone.

The reflection smiles back.

He plunges his face in the flowers, laughing at the bees that rise in consternation.

Breathing deeply of the cleansing fragrance, he follows his heart home...

***

Dinner with Vee is at the Millhouses and there is something of a gift giving too. A copy of our third book, 'Giants Dance: Rhyme and Reason' and to lighten the mood a little if it gets sombre, a fossil that Wen picked up on Ilkley Moor and which to our utter delight we soon realise is a coprolite despite Ben describing it somewhat wishfully as a hawk's claw. Vee has brought us a magnetic fridge eye each which is rather apt and mine now acts as a constant reminder for me to stay awake. She then regales us with tale after tale from her theatrical past and the evening passes far too quickly.

The morning sees us heading out to Curbar Edge, again in bright sunshine, and as we crest the rise which passes Bar Brook One I get my first glimpse of the round house shadows as we have now come to call them. It is strange, although they are only 'scorch' marks in the grass, for a split second it almost seems like the structures themselves are still there and for the first time it becomes apparent to me that the brook is part of a ritual landscape separating the 'land of the living' from the other world otherwise known as the 'land of the dead' with all the stone circles and cairns on the near side and the inhabitations on the opposite bank of the far side...

"But that would mean..."

"I know," says Wen reading my thoughts, "it means they buried Bratha on the side of the living."

"Bratha?" says Vee.

"We'll explain later," says Wen and she's probably right.

The story deserves a proper sit down... not to mention a pint...or two.

*\*\**

"We should be fine it's actually 'us' this time after all!"

Our third presentation in Glastonbury is imminent and after setting the scene, so to speak, with an overview of the esoteric terrain and then explaining a little how harmony works we are finally heading towards territory which is firmer underfoot. Ben has allowed Wen and I to split the 'Meditations' between us and we have incorporated our Enneagram mat which we utilise for rituals in the Derbyshire workshops. Even the weather has improved and as Wen and I load up the Silver Bullet with the box of books we are confronted by... sunshine!

Our first stop though is Rik's as Wen is going to be away for a couple of days she has to make sure that there will be enough accessible food-stuffs to keep him going. Still, that should be no more than a stop-off although Rik usually likes a couple of cigarettes too...

As Wen busies herself inside I decide to sit out in the sun and watch the fish in the fish pond which is always a relaxing endeavour. There is something infinitely soothing about watching fishes swimming... as I start to drift with the warm sun on my face... a note of discordance chimes somewhere in the recesses of my mind... Wen is taking longer than expected and I may have time for a little cat-nap... I notice one of the Sturgeon drift into view through my half closed eyes and the note of discordance begins to chime a little louder...

'That is strange,' I think to myself, 'don't often see the Sturgeon so close to the surface, they must be sunbathing too, catching a few rays.'

The sun beats down even hotter and my eyelids close a fraction more as another Sturgeon drifts into view, belly up, its mouth gulping in air, trailing green film from its gills.

Suddenly I am bolt upright and charging across the garden to find Wen who just happens to be on her way out to feed the fish...

"What is it?"
"It's the Sturgeon, they're suffocating!"

***

## The Third Night...

### Draumas Stiðe (A Dream of Nettle)

Sleep takes him; need and fear, both call him forth into the night.
How will they see his sacrifice, the small ones… the mortals… his children…
*his* creation?
Will they understand the magnitude of what he has given?
Can they conceive the loneliness of power?
What will he see in the mirror of their eyes?
Will they dare to thwart him after *this* gift? None other would hang for
them… pierced by his own spear….
They *will* know him… won't they?
Fear carries him across a wasteland; broken homes, broken lives pass beneath
his majesty, darkly cowering in shattered void and crumbling stone.
The flaming rune draws him on, seeing the desolation left by his passage, only
darkness where he sought to bring light.
Amid the rubble of dreams a humble flower, hooded white on needled leaves.
Drifts of painful flagellation for illusions; stinging castigation for the graven
image of Self.
Accepting the touch of its humility, the scarring fire of its embrace, he calls it
to his hand.
Fibres unravel, spiralling around him to clothe the Light of Truth in a robe of
glory...

***

…Our tour of the High Places for Vee continues. The Car Park at Curbar
Edge very kindly provides another helping of ice cream and an informative
plaque which we have somehow managed to miss until this point.

"One of the prevalent hawks in the area is called a Merlin!"
"And it's probably one of the hawks that we've been calling a sparrow-hawk."
"In the medieval hierarchy of hawking birds, the Merlin was a Lady's hunting
bird whilst the Sparrow-Hawk was a Priest's," smiles Vee.

Quite how she knows these things is beyond me.

"Is that where, 'A Kestrel for a Knave' comes from?" says Wen.

"The Boke of St Alban's," says Vee still smiling.

"Is that Boke as in toke?" say I as we move to the edge and the view out over the valley. It is more than magnificent yet somehow hard to get a firm handle on in any meaningful way short of awe and awe in my mind merely approximates distance. It is almost like being on the outside of something looking in. Vee must be reading my mind for she very kindly proffers a chapter heading encapsulating just those sentiments.

"All it needs really is a pub," declares Wen breathing in the cool air, "and it just so happens that our next look out has just that."

"Lead on, Little Grub, lead on..."

***

## The Fourth Night...

### Draumas Attorlaðe (A Dream of Betony)

Dreams shadow reality, sharing its footsteps as he passes into slumber. The nightmares come: frightful goblins leech the life from the hanging figure, as he wraps himself in isolation, seeking shelter from the ghosts of defining failure.

Fenris harries his heels, a black dog who feeds on joy.

There is no place of safety within; at every turn contempt and loathing are mirrored in his mind.

He does not know who or what he may be.

He is lost in swirling mists of dark doubt.

In the shadows the rune flares, lighting a path through sleepy meadows.

The tormentor fears the light and slinks away unnoticed.

A flower like an ear of corn: food for the forgotten soul blossoms like dawn in the fields.

He calls it to him, marvelling at its simple beauty, seeing his soul shape itself to emulate its essence, knowing love in beauty as it unfurls its petals within.

Knowing himself as he feels the world.

**The Fifth Night...**

**Draumas Finule (A Dream of Fennel)**

The night hangs heavy; shadows seem to hold him, thought explores them, layering them between body and soul; seeking the quest but fearing to leave the bastion of the mind.

Sleep calls him softly, drawing him out of the enclosing night.

He questions, seeking to understand, but the stars do not answer.

They only laugh, dancing merrily for his delight. to a tune he will not hear.

The rune-flame ignites, leading him to feathered fronds of softest green whose scent is that of childhood.

He touches a curious finger to the foliage and skin sloughs from his hand.

He calls it to him, and serpent-like sheds his skin, wriggling free of its constriction, emerging grown in beauty, freed from within himself.

He touches it to his eye and vision bursts into being, a wondrous vista of life within and around.

Colours unseen, sounds unknown become the music of the heart and tears fall like rain on the parched earth of his soul.

*** 

...Two hours behind schedule Wen and I finally climb back into the Silver Bullet and turn her aerodynamically moulded nose toward the Looking-Glass Isle.

It is not like we are late or anything because the presentation is not until evening so we have all day to get there but any chance of 'questing' on the way down is now gone and we will miss lunch with Ben. Still, I would much rather a pond full of relatively healthy fish than a pond full of dead ones.

"I can't help thinking it means something."

"A sign," says Wen, "But of what?"

"If I knew that then it wouldn't be a sign it would be statement," say I.

"Basically the pond was stagnating through a lack of oxygen."

"Will the fish be alright?"

"The little ones will be fine and so long as Rik gets the pond people out to look at it today or tomorrow he may not lose all of the Sturgeon."

"Lose them? But they were swimming about like normal when we left."

"They stress very easily but as long as we have saved, Simon, Rik will be eternally grateful."

"You've named the fish?"

"Only one of them, the Ghost Koi, he's a real character."

"How can a fish be a character?"

"He blows huge bubbles at me if I refuse to feed him."

"Wen?"

"Now."

"I know now."

"What do you now know?"

"I know what William Blake was on about."

"Everything will be seen as infinite..."

"It's not even that."

"Then what is it?"

"Everything informs everything else."...

***

...Wen drives us to the Barrel Inn, which I have to say was not really much of a surprise, to me at least, but Vee is impressed with the view, how could she not be, and impressed with the pub, likewise, but the narrative soon turns to Devil's Drop and the story of the landscape is really a prelude to our sojourn in the Queen Anne lower down the hill in Great Hucklow.

Despite having attended the Alchemy One and Two Workshops Vee has never before sampled the delights of the local pub preferring instead to quaff wine in the confines of the Nightingale Centre so it was good to be able to share the Queen Anne with her as a first and we got to sit out back in the beer garden, which Wen and I had never before done, so it was newish territory for us all.

Wen finally gets around to giving Vee the low down on Bratha and as is becoming customary for that particular story emotions inevitably become somewhat strained shall we say. It is certainly a harrowing enough account and I think Wen is keen to gain Vee's take on proceedings.

Vee ponders for a long time and when she speaks she does so slowly and with great deliberation choosing her words very carefully:

"I think... that it is... very much... a case of... One Mage... One Nation," she says and then she smiles.

It takes me a long while to get there but I manage it in the end...

*** 

## The Sixth Night...

### Draumas Mægðe (A Dream of Chamomile)
Dreams wake to fear, eternal night wraps icy fingers around the heart. Summoned by need the soul slips quietly into the shadows that veil it from itself.
Ragged wisps of affection drift and fall as he moves across the patchwork fields, black on black.
Starting at every cloud that whispers to the breeze, he wanders in search of guidance and shelter, uncertain of each step, seeking permission for being.
The rune flare lights the way, casting flame on the grass.
Each footfall crushes stars... pure white simplicity, sun-centred, fragile.
The death of flowers releases their essence, a clean, green fragrance that soothes and anneals.
Healing the heart and banishing fear.
Song rises in his breast and his spirit takes flight with the hawk of the morning.

***

..."Speaking of signs," I say indicating the hawk perched on the telegraph wire by the side of the road.
"We haven't seen a hawk on a telegraph wire since... since..."
"...Since Wayland's," I finish, "you don't think they only do that when they have a message for us do you?"

Figure 17 – 'Sentinel...'

"No, don't be daft," says Wen pretending not to see the hawk perched on a telegraph wire on her side of the road.

"Well... it appears to be starting again," say I, after we pass the third such hawk.

"What have we done?"

"I don't know, maybe it's not what we've done maybe it's what we're about to do."

Wen appears to be satisfied with that for the moment but when the 'big' hawks fly in, the Buzzards and the Kites, and start buzzing the car and landing close by on fences and in trees and in fields and in one instance on a roundabout in heavy traffic she goes one better...

"Maybe we've finally arrived in Glastonbury."

I am hoping against hope that she is right about that one.

\*\*\*

**The Seventh Night...**

**Draumas Wegbrade (A Dream of Dock)**

The day leaves him alone with the twilight, he reaches out, searching for a mind to join with his own, strengthening and supporting but without incursion.

Night calls and he follows, collecting the petals that fall from her breast.

He alone must have them, even though they wither in his grasp.

The rune flames, he counts its light, wondering what it shows.

His journey leads him to a road that winds through hill and dale, silver in the moonlight.

Beside it broad leaves silhouetted against the stars ward the serpentine path.

Here is all… nourishment and protection, healing and making.

He reaches out to grasp this too for himself.

Yet he softens as the leaves touch his flesh, the bruised sap stains his hands the colour of rebirth.

The harsh lines fade into memory and fear accepts itself, renewed and awakened to a growing soul.

**The Eighth Night...**

**Draumas Wergulu (A Dream of Crab-apple)**

The spear holds him.

So does the darkness.

Dream takes him and the spear is once more in his hand.

Around him a forest that leaves its trace upon his flesh; scraping, scarring, biting as he fights his way through the undergrowth, snarling as the branches whip back upon him as he pushes his way through.

Crossing a stream he stoops to wash away the grime… but it remains indelible, deeper than flesh.

He reaches a clearing where a single tree grows, heavy with the fruit that succeed the blush pink blossoms, soft as a maiden's cheek.

The rune burns in the bark.

He plucks the fruit, raising it to his lips.

Tart, sour, clean… hard to swallow, yet its freshness heals the illusory poison of the heart.

In its cleanliness and purity, in its sharp taste, he remembers himself, drawing his spine straight as his spear, lifting his face to the heavens.

Gone are the stains of the journey, healed the heart that bore them.

\*\*\*

...Lest this become a pub fest we decide to take Vee to Tideswell next and show her the Church there.

"The inhabitants of Tideswell refer to themselves as 'Tidzers'," smiles Vee.

The last time Wen and I visited we were fresh from our initial ordeal at Devil's Drop and although of the right date and provenance we were both a tad disappointed with our visit but as we saw at High Bradfield, sometimes these things depend on just who you are with...

And with what you have just experienced.

We enter the Church, which is a St John the Baptist and it is like walking around a candy store as a child. It is hard to credit that we have been in here before and not seen all this. As a single salutary example: the statue we thought was Melchizedek turns out to be Zacharias! We must have been comatose the last time.

"Comatose is not a bad expression for Devil's Drop," agrees Wen.

"You must let me have a closer look at that place," says Vee.

"But of course," say I, "we thought you'd never ask."

"It's on the way to the Three Stag's..." says Wen.

So it is to become a pub fest after all.

However, before pitching headlong into out and out debauchery I take time out to study the stone relief work on the pulpit of St John's. From the corner of my eye I can see Wen ushering Vee from the church somewhat unceremoniously. She has never really liked my Baptist theory and still refers to it when she refers to it at all as my 'craziness'.

Initially, I cannot believe what I am seeing because from a distance it looks just like the baptised Christ figure is actually holding the Baptist's staff but upon closer inspection, and you do have to move up very close to perceive this, it is after all the hand of the Baptist who holds the staff.

Figure 18 – '*The art of ambiguity...*'

Is this the artist's sleight of hand or deliberate obfuscation?

Whatever the conclusions, the Baptist figure as depicted in this relief is a lot, lot younger than the Christ, indeed he looks almost angelic despite his full length robe-like shirt of hair, or feathers?

\*\*\*

**The Ninth Night...**

**Draumas Stune (A Dream of Lamb's Cress)**

A final night he hangs from the Tree, a final night his own spear holds him. What dreams will come... what changes they will bring?

He fears the night.

He has hung here forever, bleeding yet content in his suffering.

And ending will be a beginning and this too he fears as the dreaming takes him.

Yet he embraces the dream, welcoming it as a lover, intimate as a shared breath.

Beneath him fields of ripened corn lie golden, almost ready for the harvest; they stretch from the western horizon to the east. A gilded kingdom that shifts, rippling like water in the breeze.

The rune flames a final time as the sun kisses the distant hills, heralding the dawn.

He knows not what he seeks.

Small, delicate, barely blooming, hidden within the corn... a few green leaves. Unprepossessing, insignificant they seem, and yet they call to him with quiet strength as he turns to gather them.

These are the last.

It is done...

"Verily, verily I say unto thee
For the healing of nations
Are the leaves of this tree."

***

...Wen has stopped the Silver Bullet at the side of the road next to a stile and is allowing Vee some time to take in the view.

The view in this particular instance is a close up of Devil's Drop.

I usually feel a trifle foolish from this distance because well, really the '...Drop' is after all just a landscape feature like any other; a little odd or unusual perhaps but a feature nonetheless, except that this time when I look at the '...Drop' I can see a whole host of skull like features erupting from out of the rock.

I think back to our last sojourn here, to our high fives... and our hugs... and our elation which now seems like pure presumption.

Then I look again at the '...Drop' and it is just a rock. Plain old rock and I start to feel silly.

Even so Vee does not take in the view for long.

She shivers as a cloud obscures the sun and draws her shawl over her shoulders:

"C'mon, let's find that pub...

Figure 19 – 'Brer Rabbit...?'

...Notwithstanding our erstwhile considerations of the Grateful Dead the last time we were here there also seems to be something of an issue with intelligent animals pending.

It might seem strange for example that a number of the trickier characters from world literature are depicted as animals.

And then there is the worldwide phenomenon of animal totems which to my mind represents yet more genius from a traditional science that simultaneously allows for differentiation *and* equivalence in a way that most religions palpably do not.

Vee said something on the way down from Curbar Edge; something important about small snakes being more dangerous than large ones because they have not yet learnt to ration their poison.

If snakes were souls she may have been making a very pertinent point about Old Souls and Young and their relative insecurities.

I think about the notion of the Trickster figure more generally and his role in the system which initially Ben and now Wen and I have also been commissioned to communicate...

I think of Don Quixote and Sancho Panza: of the non-knight who succeeds in his quest by the strength of imagination alone compassionately guided by his very effective non-squire.

I think of Wiley Coyote and the Road Runner: of the bird that does not fly but which will still never be captured...

"Of course, the *real* Brer Rabbit does not need a gun nor would he let himself be stuffed, let alone killed, or caught..." says Wen contemplating the cunningly crafted window frieze.

...And then I think of the Redoubtable Mr Punch and I am again transported back to White-Lake Promenade which looks out over pale sands that still in this point in what we insist upon calling time but which might be better served by process, amongst the echoing and bouncing yells of the sea-gulls, ofttimes can be heard to resound with the clack-clack of wooden crocodile jaws and the low growl of 'sausages'...

... A paper flyer blowing in the wind clings to my ankle.

I stoop and peel it from my trouser leg, unfurl it and read...

# '...LITTLE ACORNS...'
*A Puppet-Play Figured in Three Acts*
## FEATURING THE REDOUBTABLE MR PUNCH

## THE PUPPETS:

PUNCH
STATS-MAN (dress-coat and top-hat)
JUDY
OSAMA THE EXECUTIONER (Moor with straggly
beard, caftan and turban)

I can see the wooden booth, its canvas covers rippling noisily in the sea breeze, from my vantage point on the top promenade and the close bunch of predominantly small forms huddled before it.

I walk down to the beach and reach the back of that small huddle just as the drum rolls cease... the curtain is raised, and the cheers of the audience go up...

*Punch is busy scanning at a scanning machine.*

**PUNCH:** (*Humming*) Hi-Ho... Hi-Ho...

*He lifts a piece of paper shows it to the audience, turns, still humming, and pushes it through the scanning machine. The Scanning machine beeps.* (SFX: Beep!)

**PUNCH:** That's the way to do it!

*Punch picks up another piece of paper shows it to the audience and yawns. He turns and pushes it through the scanning machine turns and yawns again. The machine beeps.* (SFX: Beep!)

**PUNCH:** (*Mimicking*) BEEP!

*Punch turns and yawns again, turns and slowly goes to lift another piece of paper, yawning, his head lolling...*

*Enter stage left Stats-Man carrying a big stick. Punch suddenly springs bolt upright and starts scanning a lot faster. The machine goes crazy...* (SFX: Beep. Beep. Beep. Beeeeeeep!)

**STATS-MAN**: *Paces left to right front stage then stops in centre and turns to audience brandishing his big stick.*

**STATS-MAN**: (*Intoning gravely*) ...From little acorns (*pause*) grow big concerns.

*Meanwhile Punch is nodding off at the scanning machine again. His head falls on the machine with a resounding crack.* (SFX: CRACK!)

**STATS-MAN**: (*turning*) Mr Punch (*no reaction*) MR PUNCH! (*Again no reaction*) He advances towards Punch and starts to prod him with his stick: Wakey-Wakey Mr Punch!

*Punch wakes up and immediately starts scanning:*

**PUNCH**: Hi-Ho... Hi-Ho... HI-HO! ...

**STATS-MAN**: (*half turning to audience*) Mr Punch, if I catch you asleep at your post again (SFX: drum roll) then it's the GALLOWS for you my boy!

*Exit Stage right... and Curtain...*

...Blimey, Punch and Judy appear to have come on a bit. I do not remember that amount of social comment from the shows I used to half-watch as a child but then again I would probably have missed it all at that age anyway.

As the kids drift back to the booth from the ice cream van the drum roll starts up again and before long the rudimentary cloth curtain is again raised...

*Punch is busy scanning.*

**PUNCH**: (*Humming*) Hi-Ho… Hi-Ho…

*Punch looks up as if hearing something and turns to the audience.*

**PUNCH**: Oh *you're* back again eh? (*He awaits response*) I said… etc.

*Punch approaches the front stage and starts to pace left to right in a parody imitation of Stats-Man.*
**PUNCH**: Stats. Stats. Stats… and more Stats (*he starts to cackle with laughter*) Mr Punch, (*mimicking Stats-Man*) if I catch you asleep at your post again… (SFX: drum roll)… Ah Fooey!

*Punch returns to his seat and, yawning, he immediately falls asleep at the scanning machine. (SFX: CRACK!)*

*Enter Stats Man stage left. He sees Punch asleep and turns to the audience (there follows an extended sequence of pantomime jiggery pokery…)*

**STATS-MAN**: Now I've got him!

*Stats-Man rushes over to Punch setting about him with the big stick…*

**STATS-MAN**: Now I've got you… you lazy good for nothing… etc.

*Punch wakes up…*

**PUNCH**: Ow! Oh! Mr Stats-Man No Ow! etc. (*and grapples with Stats-Man. They tussle to and fro across the front of the stage… Punch eventually wrestles the stick from the grasp of Stats-Man and starts hitting him with it.*

**PUNCH**: That's the way to do it!
　　　　　That's the way to do it!
　　　　　That's the way to do it!

*Exit stage right with Punch beating Stats-Man… and Curtain.*

…Well, the audience appeared to enjoy that one however I cannot help thinking that the Redoubtable Mr Punch is about to be immersed in Stat-Cack to about neck height…

Before I have chance to stroll too far down that particular causeway the rudimentary curtain is again raised to reveal…

*…A bench (left), and Gallows (right). Punch (handcuffed) stands in dock before the bench containing Judy who has a black cloth upon her head. Osama the Executioner stands by gallows rubbing his hands and dancing round the structure.*

**JUDY**: Mr Punch…

**PUNCH**: It's a fit up!

**JUDY**: …you have been tried

**PUNCH**: Why, I never tried a thing!

**JUDY**: …and found guilty of gross misconduct…

**PUNCH**: Why, I've never conducted anything!

**JUDY**: …by the court of law gathered here today …

**PUNCH**: (*turning to audience*) you call that lot a court of law?

**JUDY**: … and by the powers invested in me …

**PUNCH**: Powers? (*Looking up and around*) What powers?

**JUDY**: … I hereby pronounce judgement upon you …

**PUNCH**: (*to audience*) she's no judge! It's the Stats-Man in disguise.

**JUDY**: …You will be taken from this place immediately and hanged by the neck until you be dead.

**PUNCH**: Oh Noooooooo!

(SFX: The death march strikes up) *as Punch is led by Judy across the front of stage and given over to Osama the Executioner.*

*Judy takes off his handcuffs and exits stage right. When Osama goes to put the noose over Punch's head it won't fit so Osama tries it on and Punch runs round the gallows and hoists Osama high in the air...*

**PUNCH**: Naughty, Naughty, Naughty. That's the way to do it!

*Curtain...*

The puppeteer, a consummate professional remains ensconced in his booth until all the children have been dragged reluctantly away by their now harassed looking parents.

'...No baby, no rolling pin, no crocodile, no dog, no sausages...' I think to myself as I take the long climb back to the top promenade, Anu would not be best pleased.

\*\*\*

# Chapter Seven:

## *"...King of the Castle..."*

"Look, I have thrown fire upon the world. And I am watching it until it blazes." – *The Living One.*

Figure 20 – '*Horus-the-Elder.*'

No one questions the concept of attributing god names to planets because the planets are bodies in space just like we are and even though they are a lot more distant we can still feel their effects here on earth.

But it is an old, old concept: it is ancient; properly ancient.

The attribution of metals to planets and hence Gods is less ancient, but by our standards this modern science is still old. What does it mean? It means that aspects of the gods are deposited in the earth, and are in us also since we comprise the earth.

We are god-like in our mercurial thought processes and our jovial benevolences.

...But what of stone?

Stone was metal before metal was discovered...

***

...You hear foot-steps on stone.
You open your mind's eye and find yourself on a large staircase climbing upwards.
You surmise that you are in a castle or a large manor house of some kind.
You continue your climb and as you reach the top of the steps you see in the wall opposite a black, brocade-curtain which is embroidered with a white circle and the six points and pathways of the Enneagram hex-a-flow.
The pattern resembles a huge bird with folded wings.
You pull back the curtain with a heavy swish and step into the room beyond.
The room is circular and has a black and white chequered floor.
You see five alcoves around the room.
Over the arch of each of the alcoves is a carved symbol in a black keystone.
You turn to look at the entrance and realise that it has divided a large alcove into two smaller ones.
The alcove to your left has a sun symbol of a circle and central point whilst to your right the alcove has a crescent moon symbol.
The light in the room gradually begins to lessen and the moon symbol starts to glow.
You feel impelled towards the alcove, walk into it, and turn to face out into the room which is now in darkness.

From the moon symbol a hologram of light is projected into the centre of the circular space...

***

"At the culminations of the Eleusinian Mysteries the celebrants were shown an ear of wheat."

"...Meaning?"

"Meaning that there is a link between vision and understanding."

"They weren't given and ear of wheat, they were shown one."

"You can look but you cannot touch."

"But your mind-can-touch..."

"The eye has to be made to grasp something it patently doesn't understand before the mind can leap across the gulf of ignorance."

Figure 21 – *'A feast of friends...'*

Wen and I are still in the Silver Bullet hurtling towards our intended rendezvous with Ben on Looking-Glass Isle.

Our journey has been punctuated by a feast of hawks of various sizes and denominations all of which, seemingly, are displaying an overwhelming desire to get in on proceedings...or alternatively to actually get in the car.

We have given up trying to understand quite why and are now merely enjoying the show.

It appears, to us at least, to bode well for the event.

"We mustn't forget to get Ben his cigar."

Ben has just turned sixty and we have promised him something of a party to celebrate. The cigar was supposed to have been purchased before we set off but because of the fish pond at Rik's we didn't have time.

"No worries, there's a cigar shop on the way to the car park."...

*** 

...The holographic beam from the moon symbol cuts out abruptly plunging the room into darkness but then a faint glow becomes discernible at the four point of the hex-a-flow.

The symbol of Mars, a shield and angled spear point becomes visible in the keystone of the alcove and you walk from the one-point of the moon alcove directly down the room to the four point of Mars, and turn to stand in the alcove facing out into the room.

From the Mars symbol a hologram of light is projected into the centre of the circular space...

*** 

...Ben is sitting in the beer garden of the 'George...' poring over his tablet when we finally arrive and after greetings and the purchase of drinks Wen wastes no time in setting about him over his latest 'indiscretion', which this time proves to be the use of an incorrectly credited photograph in one of his blog posts.

If anything the advent of Ben's foray into 'blog-land' has made their pseudo rivalry even more intense. For the most part Ben takes it in good spirit and probably looks upon it as a way to re-sharpen his teeth after retirement from the business world. He is bound to miss the cut and thrust of business and Wen at these times can be more than an adequate foil.

The two of them will keep this up now until they part and my only real concern is that such playfulness can be misconstrued by onlookers and can sometimes turn into something a little less savoury than good natured sparring.

Morgy is in the throes of a funeral which is not the best preparation for the event, perhaps, but despite our late arrival, time is still on our side and we get to run through the meditations in the newly refurbished Pilgrims' Centre which proves to be something of a joy.

There is real presence in the place and to my mind it has received the blessings that should be due to it in abundance.

*\*\**

...The holographic beam from the Mars symbol cuts out abruptly plunging the room into darkness but then a faint glow becomes discernible at the two-point of the hex-a-flow.

The symbol of Mercury, a cross surmounted by a circle surmounted by a receptive half-crescent becomes visible in the black keystone of the alcove and you walk from the four-point of Mars up the room bearing right to the two-point of Mercury, turn, and stand in the alcove facing out into the room.

From the Mercury symbol a hologram of light is projected into the centre of the circular space...

*\*\**

...Ben likes to play the Trickster and one of the ways he has found to do this is to spring surprises on people. Wen does not like surprises. This being the case the chances are that at some point during the evening there will be a set to. Ben chooses to spring his surprise in the run up to the presentation as people are gathering around the 'performance' space which we have carefully prepared. The surprise turns out to be a cunningly crafted pocket sized brochure which is beyond doubt a good idea and this Wen readily concedes whilst examining it but she then goes on to point out some typos and errors in what we are assuming is a draft version of the brochure even though Ben appears to have brought along a goodly number, presumably to hand out to people. Ben 'flips', leans in close to Wen's face and gives her what can only be described as a summary dressing down.

I quickly scan the room to ascertain the effect that this very public altercation is having on the public. Thankfully, not too many of our assembled audience are as yet paying much attention and the only lasting damage this appears to have is on Wen's visage which assumes the pallor of thunder and remains thus throughout the whole of the presentation...

***

...The holographic beam from the Mercury symbol cuts out abruptly plunging the room into darkness but then a faint glow becomes discernible at the eight-point of the hex-a-flow.

The symbol of Jupiter, a cross and half-crescent extending upwards to the left, becomes clearly visible in the black keystone of the alcove and you walk up and across the room from the two point of Mercury to the eight point of Jupiter where you turn and stand in the alcove facing into the room.

From the Jupiter symbol a hologram of light is projected into the centre of the circular space...

***

...We are back at the 'George...' in celebratory mood after the presentation although Wen for one is feeling a little less than celebratory.

"He snarled at me!"
"He's snarled at you before, just there," I say pointing to the corner chair."
"That wasn't a snarl it was a snap."
"Ben is a man," say I, "but he is also a wolf of the steppe; snapping and snarling wildly, it's just Glastonbury: it finds people's weaknesses and exposes them."
"Even so...and what's more he brought me on board, and told me specifically that it was my job to do just that."
"He probably didn't expect you to do it quite so thoroughly, but let's leave the post mortem until tomorrow we still have the Birthday Bash remember."

"I remember, but I may not be participating fully. My migraine is back."

Ah, yes, the migraine that developed just prior to the presentation...

Whatever it is that Glastonbury does, it certainly does it thoroughly.

Ben is now in deep conversation with one of the leading lights on the Glastonbury talk circuit so it as well to leave him in his element whilst he enjoys his moment. I sidle over to Morgy to discuss our options for the morrow. We are all staying over at hers tonight, as a treat for Ben's birthday and we will have most of the following day to play out in too.

"We have two options for tomorrow," says Morgy, "Stanton Drew or Stoney Littleton."
"I am familiar with Stanton Drew, although I am yet to get there, and Stoney Littleton...?"
"Stoney Littleton is a chambered tomb which it is possible to enter..."
"Like West Kennet long barrow?"
"It is similar to West Kennet but a slightly different shape, it is a lot shorter and the burial chambers are not as intricate but you can get right into the heart of it."
"Ooh that sounds good; let's do that then."...

*** 

...The holographic beam from the Jupiter symbol cuts out abruptly plunging the room into darkness but then a faint glow becomes discernible at the five point of the hex-a-flow.

The symbol of Venus, a cross surmounted by a circle, becomes visible in the black keystone of the alcove and you walk from the eight-point of Jupiter down the room bearing left to the five-point of Venus, turn, and stand in the alcove facing out into the room...

From the Venus symbol a hologram of light is projected into the centre of the circular space...

\*\*\*

"...When you strip without being ashamed,
and you take your clothes
and put them under your feet,
and trample on them like a little child,
then you will see the living one
and you will not be afraid... "

-   *The Living One.*

Figure 22–*'Wings of flame...'*

...The holographic beam from the Venus symbol cuts out abruptly plunging the room into darkness but then a faint glow becomes discernible at the seven-point of the hex-a-flow.

The symbol of Saturn, a cross surmounting an inverted crescent, becomes visible in the black keystone of the alcove and you walk from the five- point of Venus up the room bearing left to the seven-point of Saturn, turn, and stand in the alcove facing out into the room... From the Saturn symbol a hologram of light is projected into the centre of the circular space...

***

...I am standing in Morgy's kitchen contemplating the wreckage of the previous night.

The crate of empty wine bottles stands like an accusation with no basis in the reality of my head space.

I can hear Ben and Morgy in the living room discussing the route for our planned outing to Stoney Littleton.

They both sound surprisingly bright eyed and bushy tailed. I know we stayed up all night around the fire and that we retired at six o'clock in the morning and that it is now ten o'clock.

I also know that I too feel great.

I enter the living room.

"I've just had the weirdest dream."

"Oh really?" says Ben assuming innocence. "How weird?"

"Well..." say I, "we sat around the fire all night and managed to perform a miracle!"

"What kind of miracle?" says Morgy.

"We turned wine into water."...

***

...The holographic beam from the Saturn symbol cuts out abruptly plunging the room into darkness but then a faint glow becomes discernible at the sun alcove of the one-point of the hex-a-flow.

As the circle and point of the Sun symbol becomes visible in the black keystone of the alcove you walk from the seven-point of Saturn back across and up the room to your starting point but this time you enter the Sun's chamber rather than the Moon's, which started your journey, turn and stand in the alcove facing out into the room...

From the Sun symbol a hologram of light is projected into the centre of the circular space...

***

...It is certainly a beautiful day for our trip to the Long Barrow: warm and sunny.

One of the things that have become apparent from our Night Long Vigil is that whatever happens up on the Moor at Ilkley it will now no longer be an initiation.

The bonding of the Triad has already been established through our long night together...

The Barrow is reached via a bridge across a stream of running water with trailing green tendrils festooned with dragonflies, whose iridescent forms flit here and there and shoot sparkling motes of light into the bright sunshine and prove well-nigh impossible to catch on camera even for Wen's well practised eye and hand...

From there we traverse a couple of fields which gently rise to the prospect which is Stoney Littleton.

And a reassuring prospect it is too with its gently humped and moulded form, to all intents and purposes looking little different now to how it did nearly four thousand years ago...

Together, Wen, Ben and I enter the Barrow but in order to do so we have to get down on our hands and knees... and crawl...

*** 

... You find yourself back on the old, stone staircase and begin to climb to the next level...

In front of you is a curtain of black and white, patterned like two droplets of water curving, one into the other. To your left the faint light shows a long straight corridor disappearing into darkness. To your right its mate stretches out before you and disappears into bright, white light. You turn and follow the illuminated pathway. The passageway does not turn or deviate as the light before you grows stronger, spilling out of the round doorway onto the stone beneath your feet. You enter the room.

Only the shadows allow you to see, for all here is snowy white.

There is faint music in the air and the sweetness of summer, otherwise all is silence, but you are not alone. As your eyes adjust to the brilliance you perceive a misty figure seated beside a crystal brazier in which a steady flame burns with crystal clarity. You question in your mind just who this may be and a male voice answers...

"I am Fear; I see myself in the mirror of ice and am afraid.
I am Courage; I face the fear and rise beyond its reach.
I am Trust and betrayal, loyalty and deception.
I am he who fears my own unknowing and who yet believes.
I am you."

***

...Mothers squeeze us into life and then spend the rest of their days trying to convince an indifferent world that it was all worthwhile...
One of the ways they do this is by smiling...
Mother smiles and circumstances contract you out.
You would have to be pretty uncouth not to recognise it for what it is.
Women smile and the universe laughs.
'What a joy to be born.'
'What a pleasure being here.'
'I love you...?'
The first conversation I ever had I had with Ma-Ma.
Ma-Ma said, 'And who's a pretty boy then?' and I replied 'EEEGGHOOOGGGHEEHEHEE' and then spat lovingly into Ma-ma's face with shining eyes.
'Ye-es, I know,' Ma-Ma continued, proving that women understand everything, and I laughed some more in approval, looked at Da-Da and started to cry...

***

...The figure reaches out to a large, circular mirror, spinning it towards you. You see yourself, a white face not unlike the one who now watches you intently.

Across your face you see emotions chase the images of your own inner fears... You want to look away, yet you cannot.

Here, you see yourself.

Again he spins the mirror and now you see yourself warrior, armed and armoured, ready for battle with pennants flying behind you...

*** 

... But there was something the matter with Mother...

For one thing it was dangerous to go out walking with her alone.

The promenade is usually a safe enough bet. A quiet stroll, taking the air, the invigorating sea breezes...

I saw the ambulance first.

I had to be dreaming.

Its siren was wailing in my stomach.

Its flashing lights had accosted my heart beat and any moment now I would be opening up my shoulder blades to swallow more victims.

I did not want to know what was happening.

I did not want to be there but I watched, fascinated, all the same.

There he was! About half a mile off shore, his little black head, like a seal's, bobbing about, defining the sky. His friend had already made it ashore. Be-towelled and bloody and severely concussed, he was being helped into the back of the ambulance...

"He's counting waves," said Mother as the wait became intolerable, "but he'll have to go soon, he'll be tiring out there treading water."

'Counting waves? Treading water?' Mum knew everything, evidently.

I started counting waves too...

Seven and nine it seemed, were the big ones and every third cycle on nine a real monster rolled in but I would not have liked to have had to wager my life on it. The stranded man got it all wrong when he did eventually start swimming for shore. He was aiming for the steps but he had not taken the current into account. We started walking to keep up with his drift...

The moment he set off the sea invaded my stomach.

A whole ocean of water flooded my insides, its frothing, hissing loam and heaving swells, with league after league and fathom upon fathom on top of that, swilling my interior briny and green.

The moon had a hold on my lungs. It kept topping me up and draining me back out again...

After only his first few strokes the man became entangled in the seaweed of my bronchial tree.

Through a forest of sodden alveoli he groped for a straw and came away with my heart.

He tried using it as a life raft. He had tested it out, like a float, submerging it a few times, and it bobbed back up... but now his whole weight was taking it down. It could not hold his plight. It kept skipping beats as it was pummelled, dragged, rolled and scraped, dredged along the sea bed...

His first assault on the sea wall was less than successful.

He needed a footing, a grip; he needed to evade the next wave.

He just sort of slipped on the green slime and slid back into the sea.

Back into a sea which was happy to pick him up and throw him back out for more but first it swept him around in the broil a bit: a lolling tongue savouring a morsel...

Up he went again. Down he slid again after tottering along as best he could for a few feet and thumping back onto his side...

He was going to die.

The monster ninth was going to pitch him headlong into the abyss.

Mother was analysing his performance like a film critic.

Only a Herculean Escape would satisfy her expert eye.

She kept punctuating his failures with sighs of 'Well!', and tutting loudly as if affronted by the sheer absurdity of his attempts.

In between times she explained to me what he should be doing...

Mother was first to spot the blood.

"He's bleeding," she pronounced fatalistically.

It was the little growths on the sea wall which were the problem.

Those innocuous little corals and shingles were tearing his skin as effectively as a paper shredder.

The sea was grating him on the living concrete as if he were a scrawny block of cheese. It looked as though we were going to have the 'pleasure' of watching his whole body shorn away from his bones. The sea sloshed him onto the steps as if he were a wet tissue and then withdrew. I saw his senses leave his head. A bemused haze fell upon his expression. He was about to give up the ghost. He laboured to his feet and began lurching up the steps. Behind him the sea was re-amassing its might for another attack. The wave crashed down on his shoulders, forcing him to his knees. He was on the very point of collapsing backwards into the sea when he somehow propelled himself forwards and even managed a jaunty little jog to the top of the steps. Up he came...

...Up and over the 'Keep Out ' Chain.

...Up... and onto the lower promenade.

His body was a rainstorm of blood.

A thousand rivulets were running to ground, mottling his torso.

He stood like a warning... Red... A stream...

A grisly, marbled man...

***

...Once more the figure spins and the mirror catches the crystal flame, plunging the room into darkness but illuminating another doorway, a circle of light in the wall.

You turn and walk towards it, following the long, straight path, the stone is cool beneath your feet.

Darkness engulfs you.

You reach out a hand but cannot feel the walls.

Carefully, you look back...there is no light to guide you, only darkness.

Your breath sounds loud in your ears and you feel the thumping of your heart through your body.

You do not know where you are going, but keep putting one foot in front of the other, facing straight ahead.

The sound changes...

You have an impression of space around you.

"The darkness lies. You cannot see me, yet I am here. I need your eyes."

Light grows in the room, a weak, hesitant light. All here is blackness, velvets and silk. Only the faint light on their textures allows you to distinguish shape and form. You see a woman, seated before a table upon which rests a black mirror. She angles this towards a pale lamp and the light grows.

"See, I chase the shadows. I am a Mistress of Light. By my hand the darkness comes and goes." She stands, walking towards you holding her mirror before your face. You gaze into the darkened depths and see her face reflected there instead of your own.

"Foolish child, we are one, you and I, you wear my beauty, and I yours." She angles the mirror to reflect her own face, and your face gazes back. "I become what you are; you are what I see, that is the law of my mirror." As she speaks she begins to glow, changing her form and becoming your reflected image, until you stand before yourself in light and grace.

"You are what I see, and I see what you truly are."

For a moment the figure is a blaze of light then the mirror is turned and directed to a third passageway.

The room fades once more into darkness and you follow the path of light...

*** 

...I tried explaining it to Father once, about how there was definitely something the matter with Mother because of the way things turned out around her, and about the sort of things that happened when she had a hand in events... I had got as far as the bloody man on the promenade when he interrupted me. He was wearing a broad smile as though I had just uncovered a favourite but long forgotten joke of his...

"Don't worry ..." he laughed, "next time we're in town together we'll walk back home along the prom..."

Dad's answer to the irresistible horror of the sea was to let me build my very own little castle in the sand of the ocean bed along with all the other kids who were on the beach that day.

When I had finished raising my pile we climbed onto the upper promenade, leaned together on the salt scourged rails and watched the sea dissolve all our efforts.

It was too much for a lot of the other kids.

They shuffled off pretty sharp when their castles started to crumble and melt without the least sign of resistance.

They seemed eager to get back home once their walls were breached.

They left like badly trained dogs on a leash, tugging their owners at a forced pace.

Dad was not in any hurry though he would have stayed until high tide if I had let him.

He did not say anything.

He just stared into the edge of the fizzing tide... staring at the little bubbles of air which skated over the film of sand and sea, as the latter touched and fled... and then caressed... and held...

In our house when people who knew the family died, Mother cried and Father went about his daily routine unperturbed.

He sometimes looked as though he was thinking deep thoughts but if he ever did he never expressed them.

Maybe he was thinking about his mother?

Mother Sleep Mother Mead Mother Eat
Mother Need Mother Heat Mother Sin
Mother Greed Mother... Madeline? ...

***

...Another long corridor brings you back to where you began. You pass through the black and white curtain that seems to be made of alternating raindrops. The chamber is Spartan, there are few things here, yet all are stark and clear in black and white, light and shade in equal measure.

In the centre of the room stands a man dressed in the pied robes of a Jester. In one hand he holds a staff crowned by a horse's head carved in ivory, in the other a drawn sword of black steel.

"You disturb my slumber. What do you seek here?"

An answer springs into your mind; a single phrase. The Jester laughs softly as if reading your thought, "So you bring a shade and a mask, do you?"

He gestures behind you and you see an inky black shadow streaming out behind you, and in its hand it carries a mask.
"Let them go."
Confused, you look at him, not knowing how.

"Let them go," he cries.

You shuffle your feet, trying to shake off the shadow. The Jester strikes the ground with his staff. The floor ripples beneath your feet and the stone seems liquid and unstable. Yet still the shadow clings.

"Let them go," he whispers gently with a voice full of love. He raises his sword and with a mighty blow it crashes to the ground behind you. The room explodes into light and you see no more...

Figure 23 – *'Tree Spirit...?*

# Chapter Eight:

## *One Pointed Stone...*

"Jesus Christ, the Judge of Righteousness, Beasts and Dragons knew the Saviour of the World in the wilderness and came and worshipped him?"

- The Ruthwell Cross.

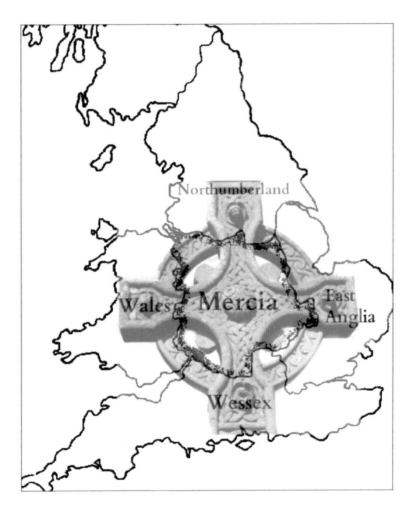

Figure 24 – '*Anglo-Saxon Realms...*'

Wen raises her now infamous left eyebrow in an arch to rival the base of the Eiffel tower and I know I am in trouble.

"Isn't there a colon missing from that quotation Mr Sams?"
"The quotation is taken from a carved stone," say I with feigned exasperation, "and so far as I am aware colons were not used on ninth century carved stones."
"Even so, it's a bit of a stretch..."
"We'll be looking at some of the other possible interpretations as we proceed but it does do one thing regardless of the interpretation one chooses to foist upon the inscription..."
"It establishes another important link between the Anglo Saxon Christ and Odin..."
"The birds and the beasts are ravens and wolves."
"But where does the dragon fit in?"
"The dragon is the spirit of the land."

\*\*\*

Ben, Wen and I are still huddled in the heart of a chambered long barrow somewhere in the heart of the Somerset landscape and I have to say for someone who is normally claustrophobic I am dealing quite well with the all-encompassing earth and stone.

Although it is quite difficult to see everything with the three of us cramped in such a small space, the surrounding rocks as well as having an incredibly secure and welcoming feel to them just like those of Wayland's Smithy, also carry the forms and images of the ancestors just like those of West Kennet Long Barrow and three out of three cannot really be an accident.

"Whose ancestors?" says Wen.

Our ancestors...

\*\*\*

...And it came to pass:
...As the Children of Men journeyed from the East,
that they found a plain in the land of Shinar:
and they dwelt there.

And they said, 'Let us build us a tower,
whose top may reach unto heaven
and let us make us a name for this plain.'

But all they had for brick was stone, and slime was all they had for mortar.

And they said, 'Let us make bricks from the stones by burning them through,' and the whole earth was of one language and one speech and one mind and the tower began to rise...

And the Lord looked down and saw the tower which the Children of Men were building and he thought to himself, 'Behold, the people is one mind, and they have all one language and this is what they do, now nothing will be kept from them which they have a mind to imagine. I shall go down to Shinar and there confound their language that they may not understand one another's speech.'

And so the Children of Men left off building the tower to each build their own separate city instead.

And the Lord scattered them abroad from thence upon the face of all the earth.

Hence that place was known as, The Plain of Bab-Ili, which means 'God's-Gate'.

\*\*\*

Wen and I are walking up the steep sided mound which constitutes the approach to Bakewell Church and the Saxon High Cross which now stands sentinel to the Church facade.

There is a riot of ravens playing hide and seek amongst the tombstones of the church yard and if Wen had been quicker with the camera she would have got a shot of one of them perched on the stone which is the focus of our visit.

Our first concern is to establish whether or not the stone was ever a cross.

Granted, the top of the stone does widen into what could possibly be regarded as the start of the base and the arms of a cross but could equally well have once taken the form of a hammer in which case it would have been Thor's hammer.

There is though also another possibility which given that the top of the stone does without question depict Odin upon his eight legged horse Sleipnir is perhaps a far more persuasive alternative...

***

...Cast out of the garden in the east, the raiment
of light fell from the bodies of Abadam and Yva.

They rested on a riverbank and brooded on
their loss of immortality, "O Abadam, have
we erred? " cried Yva but Abadam consoled
her, plucking leaves from a nearby fig tree to
serve as a covering for their nakedness...

***

... "And what alternative is this," says Wen in a somewhat accusatory tone, "you never mentioned this in any of our dispatches."
"It isn't that much of a radical departure, actually, I mean when all is said and done it is a fairly obvious idea really..."
"Stop prevaricating and spit it out," says Wen enjoying my discomfort.
"Well, I thought the stone might actually be a representation of Yggdrasil."
"You're right," says Wen, "It isn't that much of a stretch, but why would Yggdrasil have icons carved on its trunk?"
"Yggdrasil has icons carved on its trunk because the World Tree is also a

representation of time."...

***

...When Abadam and Yva had departed the garden in the east, there was a silence there about the space of one day.

To bar the way to its holy mountain so that
Abadam and Yva could never return, the Spirit
appointed a cherub with whirling limbs of flame...

***

...Wen sits down on the flat topped tomb alongside the Saxon High Stone, takes out a cigarette and starts to smoke it whilst looking out into the far distance.
Every so often she scratches her head starts to say something, thinks better of it, and looks back out into the far distance again.
When she eventually stands, she runs her hands pensively over the back of the carved stone and declares, "None of the icons are Christian are they?"

"None of the icons are Christian," I agree.
"And that's no crucified Christ on the top of the stone either."
"If that's no crucified Christ on the top of the stone what is it?"
"It's Man as the Centre of the Sun..."

***

...Wen, Ben and I are still in the centre of the womb of the earth but Wen is slowly making her way out of the entrance passage on hands and knees.

Realising that our all too brief sojourn here is about to come to an end I strike up a chanted 'Om' with rather disappointing results it has to be said.

Ben picks up on the idea and starts to chant the 'Ra-Ma' and that works really well so I join him for a time until he too turns and starts to crawl on hands and knees out of the entrance passage...

\*\*\*

...As Abadam and Yva made their way out of the garden in the
east, it seemed as though the leaves of the trees themselves
were whispering: "I will put enmity between you and the
woman, and between your seed and her offspring.

You shall bruise his head as he shall bite your heel,
and he shall bruise your head as you shall bite his heel."

But it was the serpent Abadel hissing at
Abadam from the branches of the tree of life...

\*\*\*

....Finally it is my turn but rather than go out on hands and knees I resolve to
try and get out with my soles planted firmly on the floor of the inner earth. It
is not easy by any means and it fair crucifies the back and plays havoc with
the breathing but slowly, ever so slowly I inch my way out into my new
world.

The first thing I see is Fiona sporting in the sunshine and for a moment I
entertain the notion that I have been re-born into a world of furry humans.

Fiona is Morgy's dog of course but she seems rather pleased to see me
anyway and starts trying to jump up and lick my face...

\*\*\*

...Yva followed on Abadam's heels, "O Abadam,"
she cried. "You have walked in the garden in the
east, where every precious stone was your covering.

You were a sealer of the sum, whose works and trappings were
prepared, and set all about you, on the day you were created.

You were a guardian of the holy mountain,

anointed in the shadow of the sacred tree.

You were perfect in wisdom and filled with beauty,
and you walked with the spirit amidst the stones of fire.

Yet for me you have relinquished all of this.
I will come with you, wherever you may go.”...

\*\*\*

...Morgy is lying on the top of the mound over the portal sunning herself.

I climb up to the top of the barrow using the entrance stones as steps and Fiona follows the long way round bounding up the grassy side with her lead trailing.

“There you are,” says Morgy, “you daft dog!”

Ben and Wen have retired further back on the top of the barrow and are discussing the new plans for our imminent sojourn on Ilkley Moor but they are too far away for me to hear what they are saying.

Fiona has busied herself with a blade of grass which Morgy is twisting. It seems almost incomprehensible to me that so much fun can be derived from a single blade of grass.

“I’m amazed it is still intact,” say I referring to the barrow, “You would think that the vandals would have got to it by now.”
“It’s a pretty spooky place though,” says Morgy, “especially at night.”
I ponder Morgy’s use of the word spooky which is exactly right and give silent thanks to the higher powers that I am not afflicted by such terrors.

Fiona suddenly loses interest in the blade of grass that Morgy is twisting and tries to lick my face again...with a large measure of success.

\*\*\*

...Abadam and Yva heard the Spirit calling
for Abadel as they walked in the east.

They hid themselves amongst the trees of the garden.

And the Spirit said to Abadam, "Where is Abadel your brother?"

"How should I know, am I my brother's keeper?" Said Abadam.

And the Spirit said, "O Abadam, there is no secret
which can be hidden from me, even now, the voice
of your brother's blood cries out to me from the ground.

You have lifted up your heart and said, 'I am a god,
I am stronger than my brother,' yet although you have
set your heart as the heart of a god, you are not a god but
a man, and the ground is cursed for your sake. By the sweat
of your brow shall you sow your seed, and it shall bring
forth thorns and thistles, so that you shall eat of the
herb in sorrow all the days of your life.

I will bring strangers upon you:
they shall defile your brightness,
they shall bring you down to the pit,
they shall turn their hearts against the
beauty of your wisdom, and you shall die
the death of those slain by the hand of strangers.

Will you then say to your slayer, 'I am a god,
there is no god in the hand that slays me?'"

And the Spirit banished Abadam from its garden in the east...

\*\*\*

...With something of a saliva enriched face I stand and walk further back over
the hump of the Barrow to where Wen and Ben are ensconced in the long

grass.

"We're still going to do Ilkley Moor," says Wen happily.
"But we're just going to see what the day gifts us," says Ben.
"You mean we're just going to play," say I, "That's good because that's all I ever do really."

Ben laughs heartily but something looks through my eyes and wonders whether he will be *able* to simply play without turning it into a game that must be won or lost...

*\*\*\**

...Abadam and his brother Abadel contended for the favour of Yva...

Abadam offered her sapphire while Abadel offered topaz.

Yva was pleased with Abadel and she lay with him.

The sight of Abadel and Yva coupling made Abadam jealous.

His face turned black with rage: "This world was
not created in mercy nor is it ruled by compassion."

He struck Abadel a blow with his club and killed him.

Abadel's soul escaped from his body: it flew about the scene
of slaughter and eventually settled on the tree of life, where it
assumed the form of a serpent and coiled itself about the trunk.

Abadel's blood lay bubbling and seething where it had been spilled.

"What have you done?" cried Yva.

"Look, I am a god, I am stronger than Abadel, you are
now mine alone to treasure and my heart is gladdened."
Yva yielded to Abadam and they lay together until the cool of day...

***

...After perusing the Sun-Man in the centre of his Sun-Disk Wen circles the Saxon High Stone and contemplates what the front face of the shaft or trunk is now but which was without question once the back face. It shows the roots of the tree Yggdrasil as spirals one on top of the other.

"Not your normal root system then," smiles Wen.

"Decidedly weird in fact," say I.

"More like a system of chakras in fact," says Wen.

"Or a system of centres," say I.

"The Norns, which some have insisted on equating with the Weird Sisters, presumably would be situated at the centres of the spiral root system."

"You would think..." say I kicking the base of the stone in contemplation.

"What is it?" says Wen.

"I don't know if its relevant but since we are due to go up to Ilkley Moor which you never tire of telling me has got more petro-glyphs per square mile than anywhere else in Europe."

"Well, it has," says Wen proudly.

"And that being the case I took a look at some of the Aboriginal stone art from Australia."

"And what did you find?" says Wen encouragingly.

"They painted X-Ray Men and X-Ray Cats and Dogs."

"They painted what?" says Wen.

"Well obviously not X-Ray Cats and Dogs in actual fact but rather X-Ray Kangaroos and Emu and perhaps even Witchety-Grubs."

"Careful," says Wen, she is a little delicate where grubs are concerned. "Was there a reason for them being transparent?"

"There undoubtedly was although it's not so much a case of them being see-through as such but rather actually being able to see *inside* them. There are two types of drawing too, those for non-initiates..."

"And those for the initiates?"

"Quite..."

"And the difference is?" says Wen...

***

...On the sixth day the earth was delivered of Abadam, the very
image of the Spirit conceived in the likeness of a lump of clay.

The Spirit breathed life into the clod and Abadam rose to his feet.

His head was level with the divine seat in heaven, and
as he looked about the celestial abode his huge frame
and radiant countenance, so amazed the angels that
they flocked, trembling to the Spirit: "Can there be
two divine powers, one in heaven, the other on earth?"

To calm them the Spirit placed its hand upon Abadam,
vastly diminishing his aura and greatly reducing his size.

Then it smote Abadam in half and by thus dividing
his nature, the spirit created a second man, the
twin of Abadam whom it named Abadel.

The Spirit set the twins on its holy mountain
in the east as custodians of the garden...

*** 

... "The non-initiate paintings depict the interior organs of the hunted animal
and the skeleton of the hunter who is nevertheless regarded as a non-human
spirit," say I.
"Isn't that just guilt transference?" says Wen.
"That may be one interpretation of it, yet the aboriginal hunting ritual is
incredibly precise in its delineation of the body forms and movements
required to kill, and it may also be that it is these body forms and movements
that are perceived as actually belonging to another order of being altogether."

Wen is starting to look at me gone out again but I can tell that she has made
the very obvious connection between this concept and the concept of ritual
gesture employed by the esoteric fraternities.

"...and the initiate paintings?" says Wen with some small measure of trepidation.

"The initiate paintings depict the same animals with landscape features for organs," say I.

"Take this, all of you, and eat of it," Wen muses without a second's hesitation.

***

...The Spirit planted a garden on its holy mountain in the east; it was sown with trees whose fruits were blazing jewels: diamond, sapphire, and agate, emerald, sardonyx and cornelian, opal, beryl, and topaz, malachite, garnet and amethyst.

In the centre of the garden grew the tree of life; four streams, of milk, honey, wine and oil issued from its roots:

the golden leaves and bright, crimson jewels which adorned its branches, surpassed in beauty all the other created things, and its glorious crown threw a radiant shadow over the garden.

The garden in the east was tended by Yva, the mother of all living...

***

"I'm not sure I quite 'get' how this fits with our tree," says Wen pensively.

"The icons are the 'internal organs' of the tree, and the tree is horizontal generation," say I.

"A Family Tree," says Wen.

"Our Holy Family," say I.

"The Tree of Jesse," says Wen.

"Is a Tree of Essence," say I.

"If you're not tending the tree..." says Wen.

"Then, you're in it," say I.

"Selah!" say Wen and I in unison.

***

Figure 25–'*Sun-set...*'

"In the beginning darkness
lay on the face of the deep.

All was chasm and chaos.

The Spirit spoke from the deep,
"Let there be light," it said, and
there was light, the first day.

"Let there be firmament," it said, and the
deep was divided into upper and lower,
heaven and earth, the second day.

Figure 26–'*Sun-rise...*'

"Let there be lights in the firmament of heaven,
it said, and it was so: heaven brought forth
sun, and moon, and stars, the third day.

"Let there be land and sea on earth," it said,
and it was good: earth brought forth grass,
and herbs, and trees, the fourth day.

"Let there be man and beasts, fish
and birds and creeping things," it said,
and it was very good, the fifth day...

\*\*\*

# Chapter Nine:
## *Fin Cop*

'...But of the fruit of the tree which is in the midst of the garden, ye shall not eat of it, neither shall ye touch it lest ye die...' - *Gen 33*.

Figure 27 – *'Something Egyptian...?*

To recap: first there was Wencobank...

"Don't you mean Wincobank?"

...Before Wen started infiltrating all the place names of Old Albion there was Wincobank: a harrowing enough sojourn on a hill-fort in the middle of the Field of Sheaves... And if that were not enough we then followed the trail back to the Raven Stone and from there were led to Barbrook One where three more harrowing encounters failed to dampen Wen's appetite for the quest and after we finally worked out a little of what Arbor Low was about one further harrowing encounter, for Wen at least, threw up the name Fin Cop and she wonders why I am a little apprehensive about our projected truck with what turned out to be another mammoth and I mean seriously mammoth Hill Fort.

"It's one of 'Ours'," says Wen somewhat belligerently.

First we have to find it though, and once we have found it, then we have to get to it.

"It looks like something Egyptian."...

*** 

## Of Truth and Legend IV: the Giant's Tale

The piper of Shacklow
The fiddler of Fin
The old woman of Demon's Dale
Calls them all in.

In the deep river valley, where the Wye falls and tumbles across the stones or spreads its silken surface wide, the tall mound of Fin Cop is silhouetted against the sky.
Many are the mysteries held in the heart of that hill; ancient secrets and stories that tell of love and loss.
One such is the tale of a giant named Hulac Warren, the fiddler of Fin...

*** 

They said I was born of the Balefire, when the priestesses left the enclosure to open the womb of the land as the dark time fled. I did not know, not then.

She was of the Old People, small and dark, a plump figure hunched singing over the quern. He tended the goats and fowl and life was simple. I learned the ways of hut and hearth, playing in the dirt with the dogs, my feet always stained with the green of the grass.

I do not remember that they ever spoke my name. They called me *little one* or *bright one* because of my hair and smiled, and sometimes shared glances I could not read.

Grandmother shared our hut. She never moved from her place by the fire, her hands counting stories as she muttered in the smoke-scented shadows. At night I would sit at her feet and the wizened face would come to life, telling the tales of gods and heroes, her wrinkles drawing the map of her days as they passed through her dreams.

She would sit thus, pulling the rough comb through my hair, holding me between her knees as she worked, bringing the otherworld to life and showing me the pictures in the flames until I slept.

One night she too fell asleep. I felt the life leave her as a sigh and stayed there as her flesh cooled, the spark withdrawn, until he gathered me up, dried my tears and wrapped the furs around me.

I dreamed her that night. That was the beginning.
And then they came...

\*\*\*

...Hulac lived in a cave where the limestone turrets of Hobs Hurst stand like a castle against the slope of the hill.

It is said that the giant was never seen, save by starlight when his hulking shape blocked the moon, and when, for a bowl of cream, he would thresh the corn, doing the work of ten men in a night.

Yet though he was not seen, he himself watched from his lonely castle and when the sunset gilded the hills the sound of his music could be heard on the breeze...

\*\*\*

...Acrid smoke fills the small lungs, screams in the night, drowning her whimpering, crushed beneath the silent stillness of her mother. Rigid with fear, she watches the sticky, crimson pool growing around her fingers, staining red the mark on her hand. She watches the earth drink blood.

Figure 28 – 'Hobs Hurst...'

Another scream, deeper, gurgling and she is looking into her father's eyes. He looks surprised. His mouth gapes and she sees the light flee. His throat gapes too.

The earth is drinking him also.

There is coarse laughter in the torchlight and the stench of burnt flesh.
No one comes.
Only Death...

\*\*\*

...In the valley lived fair Hedessa.

As gentle as a fawn was she, lovely as the morning, soft as the pellucid waters of the stream that laughs at the mountain's feet. Yet her voice was sweeter and she sang as she tended her father's sheep, watching over them tenderly as they strayed amongst the wildflowers.

She sang of the luminous dawn and the white of snowflakes, she sang of the velvet, jewelled night and she sang of love, for her heart was given to the scarred hunter who lived alone in the forested hills...

\*\*\*

...That was the second.
The first a memory I was yet to know.
These things come as three.
Threes are important.
I should have known...

\*\*\*

...Hulac watched from the shadows as Hedessa danced amid the trees and listened to the music of her voice and his heart was filled with love for her. One evening as the summer drew to a close he waited for her behind the wide trunk of an oak tree and when Hedessa came, leading the sheep to the stream he spoke softly.

His voice was no more than a whisper on the wind and Hedessa, looking all around, saw no-one.

"Could you love one whose face is unlike that of other men?"

"Yes," she whispered. Her love carried the mark of the boar on his cheek.

"Could you love one who loves silence and solitude?"

"Yes," she replied, smiling at the thought of the clearing in the trees far from the village.

"Could you love one who would take you away from the world?"

"Oh yes," she sighed softly, the music of the heart was in his voice and the magic of the moment caught her dreams and wove them bright.

Hulac would have spoken then, but the women from the village came laughing to the stream and he slipped away into the shadows, afraid of so many eyes. Hedessa danced on the green lawn and wove the wildflowers into garlands for her hair.

The women smiled, for she was beloved of all and they knew the song of a maid in love...

Figure 29 – 'High Pastures...'

\*\*\*

...Smoke stings her eyes; tears track grief through the paint on her cheeks.

"...Again." The voice is hard, implacable. "Further..."

She sobs and plunges back into vision, following the smoke backwards, backwards, back to that night.
It was always thus.
The visions are clear and sharp, but always the same.

And yet...

\*\*\*

...Early next morning the shepherdess led her flock into the high pastures. Her dreams had been those of a maid who stands on the verge of womanhood and her thoughts drew her eyes inward to her heart.

She climbed higher than she intended, through the deep moss and flowers, her tiny feet wet with dew and stained with the green of the grass.

Her heart was light, surely he would come again... surely he would come for her tonight?...

\*\*\*

...The sun is warm on the plateau. The kine graze, lazily swishing flies with their tails. In the little fields the old man works, the only man here on the Hill, the place of the Seers who served the gods.

They need no men folk, here on the Hill. They are safe now behind the great stone walls, protected by the steep slopes of the mound. They are safe... years untold the seers have dwelt here; respected, sought by the clans.

They weave the dream sight... and they are cherished.

Children laugh and run in the afternoon haze, young women sit outside their dwellings, plaiting veils of flowers, ready for the night. They will not be seen, the flower maids, only known by the young men they meet by flame and under the star-fire. But they will return no longer maiden. Tonight the fires will burn as the priestesses become the land.

The Eldest watches...
Her skin is a leathern apple after midwinter, her hands silent on her lap.
She watches, remembering. She had been young once, long ago.
She had served the flame and the daughter of that night wore fire in sleek braids that fell to her waist.
Tonight they would be unbound and she too would take the veil and venture into the night.

A smoke and fire scented night... the fragrance of crushed flowers clings like memory to her skin. She folds her hands over her belly and smiles...

\*\*\*

...At noon the sun shone bright and Hedessa sought the shade of the rocks of the ancient place where few now came.

Melancholy tales were told of this place, but no sadness could cast its shadow on the heart of a maid in love.

She had walked far in her daydreams and rested, looking down on the turrets of the giant's castle far below.

None ventured there.

They accepted his service in the night but shunned the twisted creature.

They said he was a demon.

Hedessa looked down on his cavernous home and shivered.

Then she closed her eyes and smiled; her hunter would protect her from demons...

\*\*\*

...Their fires light the horizon.

She counts them, holding the small child close, crooning softly over its head.

She had counted them when they first appeared.

She watched them every night, long before eyes could see them.

She watched them with the dream-sight.

And the fear had come.

The woman, plump and dark, one of the Old Ones, holds out her arms, fear and compassion in her eyes; milk in her breasts from her own lost bairn, she takes the child.

A small hand reaches up, marked; she catches her breath and looks up meeting the young woman's eyes.

A wordless smile, a nod.

The mark of the Seers.

Folding the shawl around the babe, she closes her eyes for the blessing then disappears into the night...

\*\*\*

...As if she had conjured him with her daydreams she heard his voice calling

softly, "Hedessa…."
Then closer he called… and closer still.
A shadow stole the warmth of the sun and Hedessa opened eyes filled with love. Yet it was not her hunter who loomed over her, but the twisted figure of the giant, Hulac Warren.
Love turned to fear...

*\*\**

…They walked far that night, trailing the goats behind them, following the stars and the hidden valleys… man and woman, Grandmother riding the ox with the borrowed babe in her arms.

It would be many nights …from the Snake to the Raven's lands, seeking shelter.

The sickness gnaws as the images unfold.

She tries to turn from them, follow the journey of the little one, but the vision blazes in a memory that is not her own but that of her kin...

*\*\**

…Hedessa screamed and the sound echoed across the hills.
Those in the valley looked up and saw the two silhouetted against the sky. Neither those who watched from below nor the shepherdess herself saw the hope in the giant's eyes turn to pain.
They did not see his tears as he reached out his hand, helpless to speak before the revulsion in her gaze.
Could she not love him? No. She could not, would not.
The man she loved was tall and straight, not gnarled as old stone, bent as the willow. Yet he wept and reached out to her. Hedessa turned to run and tripped on a fallen stone. Hulac pounced to save her from the fall but in her fear she struggled and anger took him. Not at her, but at himself and at a world that reviled those whose form reflected another realm...

*\*\**

...Screaming, running, smoke and blood.

Children spitted like rabbits, flung from spears... dying as they fall.

Or not.

Left to bleed, slowly, in pain and fear on the steep slope.

Eyes trampled underfoot. These were the Seers.

Noise, stench of smoke, faeces and roasting meat...

Thatch blazing in the night; a beacon of grieving, a pyre of memory.

Coarse laughter.

Hands crushed underfoot by those who watch, who wait their turn.

Arms that fought, broken and useless.

No escape, naked and beaten; another and another.

Breasts that ooze milk now suckle horror.

Red braids fought over by human dogs in the firelight, their owner prays for death.

Another... and another.

No veil of flowers.

No bright morning.

The Eldest watches through blind sockets, her hands on her belly, life oozing from the severed wrists...

***

...And so it was that as she struggled, crying the name of her love, Hedessa tore free of Hulac's grasp and fell to her death, dashed upon the rocks below.

The cry of the grieving giant rent the air and the rocks split asunder.

They found her broken, breathing her last.

She spoke of stone.

They did not understand.

Around the place where she lay they built a circle and covered her with earth and flowers; a pale shadow of her beauty.

From the ground came water, warm as a maiden's tears and to this day the spring bears her name...

***

They had been ready. They were many.

The kine had been brought in, the gates closed, the fires raised.
The beacon lit:
Too late for help;
Scarce enough for warning.

They were women.
Priestess and seer, old and young.
Children.
They could not fight.
But they tried.

They came at night, silently. My people were slaughtered like pigs.
And worse.

None remained.

They burned their homes.
Smashed the altar.
Took the sacred flame to the thatch.
Flung them in the ditch, dead and living dead; broken.
Discarded.
The walls of the sanctuary thrown down upon them, breaking them.
And then they left.

There was nothing here for them. Only a power they feared.
A gift destroyed.
Despoiled.
Broken.

But not quite.
They failed.
A spark remained.
*She* did not die.
Broken, bloodied, used…

She woke on the rocks of the hillside and, slowly, carried their deaths to the
sacred hill, flame to flame.

Lætha… my mother.

And I remain.

I carry their souls.
Theirs too.
For the children.
For the cruelty.
For brightness lost.
For my sisters.

The earth mourns, shrouded in barren silence.
It waits to spill its secrets in the lap of the gods.

That was the first time.
The third you know.
You *saw*, little sister.
You were *there*…

\*\*\*

…Giant Hulac watched, cursing the gods, cursing hope and cursing himself.
That night he crept down to the spring to lay flowers by Hedessa's grave and his tears mingled with the waters.
When the huntsman came he did not run.
The spear pierced his flesh, but he did not die.
He cried out then to the gods to take him, in anger or anguish at the ruin of beauty; to let him lie beside her at least in death.
He did not die when they stoned him.
But the rocks drove him into the stream and there the gods took pity on Hulac Warren, turning his hunched form into an island of stone.
He rests there still, close to his love, separated from Hedessa only by the ever-running tears of the hills.

\*\*\*

…He found her alone, waiting, amid the bodies.

Calm.

The little village decimated by the raiders; her home in ashes, her family charred corpses.

The brown of dried blood on the whiteness of her hands.

They had Seen.

She smiled up at him Knowing.

He knelt before her, and she lifted her arms.

He cradled the small body to his chest.

Silent tears fell from the Guardian's eyes as he carried her to the sacred hill.

\*\*\*

*Wind whips the tears from my eyes as I listen to the whispered words; unspoken, unheard, yet present in every atom of knowing. She had waited, beyond time, beyond death, for ears to hear, and a heart open to the song of the souls she bore. I knew her well. I don't even know if she exists. Yet, we are kin, she and I. Perhaps it is I who do not exist…perhaps I am no more than the memory of her future…*

\*\*\*

…And all that is before we even get up on to Fin Cop which may have to wait now until the next book… perhaps I should explain:

"The reason why Fin Cop is not sign posted… anywhere is because there is currently no public access…"

You think such a minor consideration is going to deter Wen?

"Who *is* Fin anyway," she asks as something of an aside as we are hurtling along the tree-lined valley in the Silver Bullet with Fin Cop on our left though we do not at this point quite realise it even though we are both feeling extremely nauseous.

"Fin my dearest Wen-dull-berry," she hates it when I muck about with her name, "Fin is none other than the legendary Irish Mythological hero upon whom the Robin Hood stories are based."

"Well in that case, we're in the right part of Derbyshire for one of his Hill-Forts," says Wen with not nearly enough respect or due reverence for my copious knowledge of traditional Irish literature.

"He has a whole mythological cycle named after him, The Fenian Cycle."

"Well now you're just being boring... Bore-Don... Bore-Don..."

'Bore-don-Bore-don,' I suppose I asked for that not that there will be anything at all boring about what Wen has planned for the assault we are about to make on Fin Cop or rather our imminent incursion *into* Fin Cop but for that... we will just have to be patient..

In the meantime, there's a little bit more...

***

## Little Grub...

...Dreamt herself a butterfly
Flitting and fluttering about happily...

When she woke up she did not know whether she was a little grub who had
dreamt herself a butterfly or a butterfly dreaming herself a little grub...

There must be some difference between Little Grub and a butterfly?

It is called the Transformation of Things.

# Numbers

Fourteen stations (XIV)
Forty-Two figures (ILII)
Seven Female figures (VII)
Thirty-Five Male figures (XXXV)
Twelve Living figures of Jesus (XII)
Two Dead Bodies (II)
Four named figures (IV)
Four Hooded figures (IV)
Four Roman Soldiers (IV)

## Mysteries

Jesus is not called Christ.
The Women of Jerusalem are not so called.
Jesus' mother is not named.
Veronica is the only female figure named.
Joseph is not named.
Simon is the only other male figure named.
There is no Spear, Vinegar or Gall.
There is no Dicing for the Robe.
The Robe is draped upon the Cross.

## Symbolism

Jesus retains his golden halo in death.
On being stripped Jesus' right palm faces outward his left palm inward.
Joseph first appears holding a scroll.

Jesus appears to be scourged every time he falls.
Joseph's hierophantic gesture appears to raise Jesus from the cross.
The INRI scroll only appears on the cross that crucifies Jesus.

Joseph remains robed and hooded throughout.
The cloth that Veronica uses to wipe Jesus' face retains his mirror image.
Jesus is placed in a three-tiered tomb.

# Apocrypha

In the canonical Gospels:

Jesus does not fall with the cross.
Jesus does not meet his mother.
Veronica does not wipe Jesus' face with a cloth.

The pieta too also appears to be an embellishment of the gospel tradition
where Joseph of Arimathea deposes Jesus from the cross.

Simon of Cyrene does though help Jesus carry the cross.
There is also a Gnostic Gospel that insists that Simon goes onto take Jesus'
place on the cross and is crucified in his stead.

# Origins

The stations were originally the stopping points of a seven-fold reparatory pilgrimage from the tomb of Jesus to the house of Pilate.

The original icons showed; Jesus carrying the cross,
Jesus falling for the first time,
Jesus meeting his mother,
Veronica wiping the face of Jesus,
Jesus falling the second time
And Jesus nailed to the cross...

...A Week of Sorrows.

SIMON OF CYRENE HELPS JESUS

# Development

Pilgrims of the Sorrowful Way preferred to follow in the footsteps of Jesus.

Six more iconographical representations were added during the middle ages:
Simon of Cyrene helping Jesus to carry the cross,
Jesus meeting the women of Jerusalem,
Jesus falling a third time,
Jesus stripped of his garments,
Jesus dying on the cross,
And Jesus taken down from the cross...

...A Fortnight of Sorrows.

## Considerations

The fourteen-fold pilgrimage in Jerusalem was split into two distinct groupings some distance apart: of nine and five stations respectively.

The entombment and condemnation scenes form a pair.

The three falls with the cross and the nailing, death and deposition form natural triads.

The Joseph scenes and those featuring female figures form natural quaternaries.

The stripping and entombment do not depict the cross.

A three-figured Resurrection would necessitate the omission of Jesus.

VERONICA WIPES THE FACE OF JESUS

## Speculations

The stations are the work of the early Jesuits.

The falls were diversionary and designed to separate the Daughters of Jerusalem episode from the figure of Simon in the minds of the faithful.

The Veronica was specifically designed to counter claims made for the Turin Shroud.

The veil of Veronica may be regarded as depicting an 'imago' of Christ.

There are nine steps to Golgotha.

The figures stripping Jesus are performing an initiation.

The robe draped upon the cross is significant.

JESUS IS STRIPPED OF HIS GARMENTS

## Questions

If the story of Jesus is historical then why contemplate unhistorical episodes of that story?

Why would the Roman soldiers coerce Simon into helping carry the cross?

To what does the prophecy uttered by Jesus to the Women of Jerusalem refer?

What do the hieratic gestures of the hooded figure signify?

What do the colours of the women's robes signify?

Why does it take two people to strip Jesus?

Why is one of them bare headed and the other not?

JESUS IS NAILED TO THE CROSS

## Contemplations

A Week of Sorrows is a cycle.

A Fortnight of Sorrows is a bi-cycle.

The three falls of Jesus echo the three deaths of Merlin.

The haloed female figure may not be Jesus' mother.

Joseph may be shown hooded for a reason.

The robe draped cross resembles the mast and sail of a boat.

The hooded figure may not be Joseph of Arimathea.

The figure helping to carry the cross may not be Simon of Cyrene.

The figures may depict aspects of the personality.

## Meditations

What aspects of the personality could be represented by?

...The Hooded Figure
...The Bearer of the Cross
...The Haloed Female Figure
...The other female figures
...The figures disrobing Jesus
...The figure of Jesus
...The body of Jesus
...The figures entombing the body.

## Visualisations

Imagine the events represented by the icons playing out like a cinematic film
in your mind's eye.
Clearly visualise all the depicted figures as they are given and what happens to
them as the cinematic story proceeds.
If some of the figures appear to flit in and then out of the scenes re-arrange
the scenes so that their appearance is consistent with a design and purpose.
When the story is complete run and re-run it from start to finish.
Imagine being each and all of the figures in turn.
At the end of this process imagine being an objective observer of events.

## Proverbs

You are like a fruit picker who loves the fruit but hates the tree.

You examine the face of heaven and earth without recognising
the one who is in your presence,
for you do not know how to examine the moment.

Know what is in front of your face,
and what is hidden from you will be disclosed.

What you look for has come but you do not know it.

The one who knows all but lacks the self is utterly lacking.

Come to me for my yoke is easy and my mastery gentle...

Here ends, 'Dark Sage':
The second book of the Doomsday Triad

The story continues...

... In

# Doomsday:

# Signs of Albion.

If you have enjoyed this book please consider leaving a review.
To contact the authors or to stay up to date with news of the books and
upcoming events, please request our newsletter by emailing:
suevincent@scvincent.com
You can also find us on Face book as Silent Eye Authors,
on Twitter @SCVincent
and on our website: www.franceandvincent.com

## About the Authors

Stuart France – writer and mystic; author of *The Living One* and *Crucible of the Sun*. Stuart has a deep and practical knowledge of the Western Mystery Tradition, having followed a Path that has taken him hopping through the branches of the Trees of Knowledge and Delight. His astonishing work with symbolism and the interpretation  of myth comes from a profound understanding and love of life and humanity. After gaining his BA in Philosophy and Literature, and his MA in Writing, this Child of Light studied with OBOD, AMORC, and the Servants of the Light and is a Director of The Silent Eye School of Consciousness. He declines all responsibility for this introduction. *"I blame Wen….."*

 Sue Vincent is a Yorkshire born writer, esoteric teacher and Director of The Silent Eye. She has been immersed in the Mysteries all her life. Sue maintains a popular blog Daily Echo at www.scvincent.com and is the author of *The Osiriad* and *Sword of Destiny*. Sue lives in Buckinghamshire, having been stranded there some years ago due to an accident with a blindfold, a pin and a map. She has a lasting love-affair with the landscape of Albion, the hidden country of the heart. She is currently owned by a small dog who also blogs.

The friendship of Vincent and France has a peculiar alchemy of humour, scholarship and vision that has given birth to several books, including *The Initiate, Heart of Albion* and *Giants Dance*.

The Silent Eye is a modern Mystery School that seeks to allow its students to find the inherent magic in living and being. With students around the world the School offers a fully supervised and practical correspondence course that explores the self through guided inner journeys and daily exercises. It also offers workshops that combine sacred drama, lectures and informal  gatherings to bring the teachings to life in a vivid and exciting format. Full details of the School may be found on the official website, where there is also a forum open to all: www.thesilenteye.co.uk

# THE INITIATE:

### Adventures in Sacred Chromatography

## Sue Vincent & Stuart France

### Foreword by Steve Tanham

*Book One of the Triad of Albion*

Imagine wandering through an ancient landscape wrought in earth and stone, exploring the sacred sites of peoples long ago and far away in time and history. The mounds and barrows whisper legends of heroes and magic, painted walls sing of saints and miracles and vision seeps through the cracks of consciousness.

Now imagine that the lens of the camera captures a magical light in soft blues and misty greens and gold. A light that seems to have no cause in physical reality. What would you do?

If you were open to the possibility of deeper realities, perhaps you would wish to explore this strange phenomenon...something two people came to know as sacred chromatography.

The Initiate is the story of just such a journey beyond the realms of our accustomed normality. It is a factual tale told in a fictional manner. In this way did the Bards of old hide in the legends and deeds of heroes those deeper truths for those who had eyes to see and ears to hear.

As the veils thin and waver, time shifts and the present is peopled with the shadowy figures of the past, weaving their tales through a quest for understanding and opening wide the doors of perception for those who seek to see beyond the surface of reality.

Over 60 Full Colour Illustrations

# THE HEART OF ALBION:

Tales from the Wondrous Head

## Stuart France & Sue Vincent

*Book Two of the Triad of Albion*

**"If I am consciously following a woman who is about to engage a Llama in conversation, which I certainly appear to be, it does not impinge too negatively upon my thought processes."**

What do Jack and the Beanstalk have to do with a spiritual quest? What, for that matter, is the nature of the relationship between Salome and the Jester? Why is Wen conversing with a llama in the Yorkshire Dales? And what links the beautiful and sacred landscape that is the Heart of Albion with Breakfast in Slug Town? These, and many other questions, must be considered as Don and Wen continue the journey begun in The Initiate exploring the shadowy roots of the ancient myths and legends of these Blessed Isles, steering a perilous path through the murky waters of religious symbolism and iconography.

**"Breakfast in Slug Town?"**

Join them on their continuing quest for knowledge and understanding as they explore the landscape of England and people it with strange creatures and even stranger theories, using sacred intent and guided imagination to penetrate into the mysteries unfolding before them.

Illustrated in full colour throughout

# GIANTS DANCE:

## Rhyme and Reason

## Stuart France and Sue Vincent

*Book Three of the Triad of Albion*

It began with a walk over the bracken covered hillsides of Derbyshire to a lonely stone circle, almost forgotten. It was just a walk...until the hawk flew from the tree and once again the visions began.

Plunged into a realm beyond reality, further than history, deeper than time, Don and Wen begin to unravel the hidden messages hidden in plain sight, concealed by habit and acceptance, and extraordinary magic framed within the small things of ordinary life.

Follow a journey across the Heart of Albion and become an Initiate of the mysterious verity of verse.

*"Interesting that they should seek to make the seven four like that."*

*"Three harmonic pairs and a jubilant head?"*

*"It reminds me of something biblical."*

*"It wouldn't be Jubilees would it? The Hebrews, you know, took an awful lot with them when they fled from Egypt."*

*"I know, but it's not Jubilees, although that does bear some consideration. It's the three-score years and ten! It's precisely the same dynamic. In fact, we even raised the question of whether there was anything in the tradition appertaining to it."*

*"And now we have our answer!"*

*"The Hebrew's Divinely sanctioned earthly span of life is determined by the Seven Hathors."*

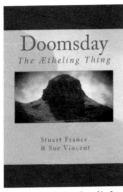

*Book One of the Doomsday Triad*

# Doomsday:
# The Ætheling Thing

### Stuart France & Sue Vincent

### "Who was this Arviragus bloke anyway?"

Don studies the light as it plays through his beer, casting prisms on the table. How is it possible to hide such a story... the hidden history of Christianity in Britain? Oh, there are legends of course... old tales... Yet what if there was truth in them? What was it that gave these blessed isles such a special place in the minds of our forefathers? There are some things you are not taught in Sunday School.

***

"Get this... 'ætheling' from O.E . . . . Æpling, 'son of a king, man of royal blood, nobleman, chief, prince, king, Christ, God-Man, Hero, Saint...'"

"Wait a minute... wait a minute... give me that last bit again."

"...Christ, God-Man, Hero, Saint..."

"Didn't we call our Arthur, Aeth in, 'The Heart of Albion'?"

"We did."

"And didn't we set his story in Mercia?"

"We did."

"Well that's it then...The Anglo Saxon kings were claiming divine descent."

"That's true, but the Anglo-Saxon kings' descent wasn't from God it was from Christ."

"And how did they get there?"

"They got there from their very own High One who also hung from a tree with a spear in his side... screaming."

"Odin!"

"They evidently regarded Christ as an avatar of Odin."

"Blimey, you'll not read that in any history book!"

"Just as well we're not writing a history then isn't it?"

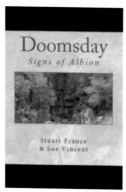

# Doomsday: Signs of Albion

### Stuart France & Sue Vincent

...."Just make sure there's enough room in the boot of the car," says Wen and throws me the keys to the Silver Bullet before disappearing back into the flat to retrieve something.

I peruse with some consternation those contents: a wheel-barrow, a spade, a crow bar and a length of rope and when I look up to remonstrate with Wen she appears to be clad head to foot in black, wearing a black balaclava on her head, and holding an air rifle.

"What the..."
"Just put that in the boot and get in the car," she says, handing me what can only be my own black balaclava and cladding.
"There had better be a damn good reason for all this," say I clambering into the front seat.
"Too right there should," intones Ben's familiar drawl as he emerges upright from his prostrate position along the back seat of the Silver Bullet.

Somewhat un-reassuringly he also appears to be wearing a black balaclava....

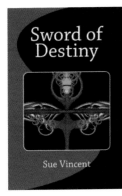

# SWORD OF DESTINY

## Sue Vincent

**"...and the swords must be found and held by their bearers lest the darkness find a way into the heart of man. Ask the waters to grant guidance and tell the ancient Keeper of Light that it is time to join battle for the next age."**

Rhea Marchant heads north to the wild and beautiful landscapes of the Yorkshire Dales where she is plunged into an adventure that will span the worlds. The earth beneath her feet reveals its hidden life as she and her companions are guided by the ancient Keeper of Light in search of artefacts of arcane power. With the aid of the Old Ones and the merry immortal Heilyn, the company seek the elemental weapons that will help restore hope to an unbalanced world at the dawn of a new era.

"Sue writes with a real grasp of the human side of people which is expressed in the personalities of her heroes and the recognizable characters that they interact with. The power and essence of her story is found in the admixture of her undoubted love of Yorkshire, her ability to see the warm and the good in all people, and her knowledge of the magical forces one can find at work in such places and between such folk. An inspired piece of writing that keeps your attention until the very last page."

*Dr G.M. Vasey, author of "The Last Observer" and "Inner Journeys: Explorations of the Soul", co-author of "The Mystical Hexagram: The Seven Inner Stars of Power".*

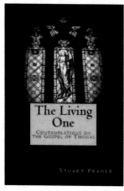

# THE LIVING ONE:

### Contemplations on the Gospel of Thomas

### Stuart France

**"...It is like the smallest of seeds and if it falls on prepared soil, it produces the largest of plants and shelters the birds of heaven..."**

Many scholars believe that the Gospel According to Thomas preserves a glimpse into the oral traditions of the Gospels. The book is a collection of sayings, parables and dialogues attributed to Jesus and forms part of the Nag Hammadi Library, a collection of ancient papyri found near the Dead Sea in 1945.

In this unique interpretation Stuart France brings the oral tradition to life, retelling the Gospel in his own words, in the way it may have been shared around the hearth fires of our forefathers. Deeply entwined with the story is the personal journey to understanding, following it down some rather unusual pathways. It begins with a road trip in an arid landscape far from home; a journey that led through a country that captured imagination and set it to music. It ends with an ancient story, told as you have never read it before.

**"Look, it's obvious, mozzies are God's Angels in disguise."**

Accompanied by a commentary which draws upon the esoteric traditions of the Mystery Schools, The Living One provides a new window on an age old story, being a transmutation of the spirit of the words, born of the personal realisations of a seeker after Truth.

> **"Salome said to Joshua, "Who are you mister, you have eaten from my table and climbed on to my couch as if you are a stranger ?""**

*Photography by Sue Vincent*

# CRUCIBLE OF THE SUN:

## The Mabinogion Retold

## By Stuart France

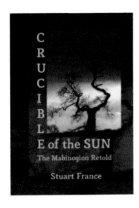

*"I will dazzle like fire, hard and high, will flame the breaths of my desire; chief revealer of that which is uttered and that which is asked, tonight I make naked the word."*

Once upon a time we gathered around the flames of the hearth and listened to tales of long ago and far away. The stories grew in the telling, weaving ancient lore whose origins lie somewhere in a misty past with tales of high adventure, battles, magic and love. In Crucible of the Sun this oral tradition is echoed in a unique and lyrical interpretation of tales from the Mabinogion, a collection of stories whose roots reach back into the depths of time, spanning the world and reflecting universal themes of myth and legend.

These tales capture a narrative deeply entwined through the history of the Celtic peoples of the British Isles, drawing on roots that are embedded in the heart of the land. In Crucible of the Sun the author retells these timeless stories in his own inimitable and eminently readable style. The author's deep exploration of the human condition and the transitions between the inner worlds illuminate this retelling, casting a unique light on the symbolism hidden beyond the words, unravelling the complex skein of imagery and weaving a rich tapestry of magic.

*Photography by Sue Vincent*

*'The author's creative and scholarly engagement with the material and enthusiasm for the original tales is evident throughout.' The Welsh Books Council*

*'I found it very inspiring!' Philip Carr-Gomm, Chosen Chief, Order of Bards, Ovates and Druids (O.B.O.D.)*

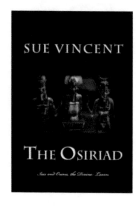

# THE OSIRIAD

## Isis & Osiris, the Divine Lovers

### Sue Vincent

"There was a time we did not walk the earth. A time when our nascent essence flowed, undifferentiated, in the Source of Being."

In forgotten ages, the stories tell, the gods lived and ruled amongst men. Many tales were told, across many times and cultures, following the themes common to all mankind. Stories were woven of love and loss, magic and mystery, life and death. One such story has survived from the most distant times. In the Two Lands of Ancient Egypt a mythical history has been preserved across millennia. It begins with the dawn of Creation itself and spans one of the greatest stories ever to capture the heart and imagination. Myths are, by their very nature, organic. They grow from a seed sown around a hearth fire, perhaps, and the stories travelled the ancient highways, embellished and adapted with each retelling. Who knows what the first story told?

In this retelling of the ancient story it is the Mistress of all Magic herself who tells the tale of the sacred family of Egypt.

"We have borne many names and many faces, my family and I. All races have called us after their own fashion and we live their stories for them, bringing to life the Universal Laws and Man's own innermost heart. We have laughed and loved, taught and suffered, sharing the emotions that give richness to life. But for now, I will share a chapter of my family's story. One that has survived intact through the millennia, known and remembered still, across your world. Carved in stone, written on papyrus, I will tell you of a time when my name was Isis."

# NOTES FROM A SMALL DOG

## Four Legs on Two

### Sue Vincent

"He asked me what it is with balls...why I love them so much. I had a think about that. It is 'cause they fly. Like birds. I'm supposed to chase birds. I am a bird-dog. 'Course, she won't really let me. It doesn't stop me barking at 'em and seeing 'em off from my garden. But it isn't the same. Somewhere, deep inside, I know what I am supposed to do, what I am supposed to be. But I can't be that for some reason... things aren't quite set up right for me to chase birds all day and bring them back to her. On the other hand, that's who I am...and you can't be anything else than that... so the balls let me be myself in a world where I can't catch birds all day.

She says that's not unusual... She seems to think that we all know who we really are, deep down, and that we spend all our time trying to find a way to be that in a world that doesn't quite seem to fit. We either find other stuff to express it...like balls.... Or we try to be what others think we should be... But you can't be a terrier if you are a retriever, can you? A bit like asking a fish to climb trees. It can be done, but it isn't easy!"

Ani, a very familiar spirit, was named for one of the ancient gods. It should, I suppose, have been no surprise when she took over the keyboard and began to write. A year later she had me collect her writings into a single volume at the insistence of her fans... who have been taken by her playful love of life and her odd wisdom...largely because she is saving for an automatic tennis ball launcher. The book is a collection of Ani's periodic posts. She even lets me write occasionally... By this time you may, of course, think I am barking mad myself... you may have a point... but I stand with Orhan Pamuk, "Dogs do speak, but only to those who know how to listen."

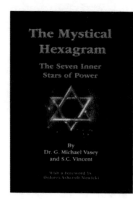

# THE MYSTICAL HEXAGRAM:

## The Seven Inner Stars of Power

## Dr G. Michael Vasey & S.C. Vincent

## Foreword by Dolores Ashcroft-Nowicki

The Mystical Hexagram is a new book by Dr G. Michael Vasey and S.C.Vincent. The book explores a symbol. Not from some scholarly or deeply complex perspective, but seeing it as a representation relating to life and living. The forces and pressures that are associated with the hexagram are, after all the forces of life at both practical and Universal levels. By exploring and beginning to understand the symbol, we are able to learn and discover more about ourselves.

The meditations throughout the book take you on an inner journey of exploration, discovering the parallels between the self and the greater reality within which we live our lives. They illustrate the connection between the inner and outer world of the self and the cosmic forces of Creation. Having traced that connecting path, the meditations offer a practical way of applying that understanding.

In addition to the exercises the book includes two very special meditations, The Garden of Remembrance and the Circle of Healing. These two you will want to revisit many times, taking away from the experience a sense of peace and beauty.

The book is now available through Datura Press

# THE SONG OF THE TROUBADOUR:

## A Silent Eye Workbook

## by Steve Tanham

*Foreword by Sue Vincent*

*With contributions from Stuart France and those who were there to share this very special journey.*

"Being is without beginning and end. This flowing, loving, intelligence is the basis of everything we know. Whatever level of consciousness we attain, it will only reveal the greater and greater depth of Being that has always been there within us and before us.

Being also forms the objects that we believe are separated from us. But the Reality and the Truth are that we live and have our own being in a sea of endless loving energy that is our true home. There is no separation, there is in the end, no journey; there is only realisation, and seeing. What unveils itself before us was always there."

A group of pilgrims have been brought together in the ancient monastery of the Keepers of the First Flame. Unexpectedly, the door opens and into their midst stride the Troubadours, holding a Child by the hand…. a very special Child in whom the Light of Being shines clear… and who can see the world as it really is…

Thus began the inaugural weekend that saw the Birthing of the Silent Eye, a modern Mystery School. This workbook is both a practical transcript of the dramatic rituals of that weekend and the story of that Birth. The book opens a window onto the workings of a modern Mystery school, sharing the accounts of some of those who attended the weekend as well as the detailed script of the powerful ritual drama. If you have ever wondered what really goes on… this book is for you.

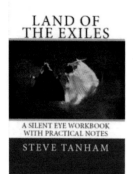

# Land of the Exiles

## A Silent Eye Workbook

## With Practical Notes

## By Steve Tanham

In April 2014 the Silent Eye, a modern Mystery School, hosted the Land of the Exiles as a weekend workshop. These annual gatherings attract people from across the world to share a unique approach to the spiritual journey that is taken by all. Over the course of the workshop a story unfolds, dramatic and emotive, engaging the hearts and minds of the participants, shadowing forth the challenges of the inner journey to awakening. This workbook includes the script from that journey, along with practical and explanatory notes, as well as the personal accounts of some of the Companions who shared an epic journey of the imagination as a spaceship crash-lands on a far-flung planet, and a cyborg forces them to play out the story of the ancient gods of Egypt, intent of calculating just what it means to be human…

The Hawk has crash-landed on the planet Idos, the crew awake from cryogenic sleep to find that their captain is missing and the ship has been taken over by a cyborg who bends them to his will, making them play out the stories of the ancient gods of Egypt as it seeks to understand what it is to be human. Their only hope of survival lies in the strange touch of the Midstream, and their own inner hearts.

A practical guide to a fully scripted ritual workshop from the Silent Eye, a modern Mystery School.

Made in the USA
Charleston, SC
11 March 2016